Disclaimer

The authors and publishers of this book acce[...] damage or loss that may arise from the use o. ... information and examples in this book. Each user is responsible for ensuring compliance with copyright, citation rules and other legal requirements.

It is the responsibility of each individual to familiarize themselves with the respective rules and regulations of their university, college or school and to clarify which procedures are legally permissible and which are considered plagiarism. The contents of this book are for informational and educational purposes only and should in no way be construed as direct recommendations for writing academic texts. The examples shown are merely intended to offer suggestions and illustrate the various aspects of academic writing with ChatGPT.

The authors and publishers assume no liability for the accuracy, completeness and timeliness of the information and examples contained in this book. It is the responsibility of each user to carry out additional research and to critically scrutinize the information presented in this book.

Contents

Introduction

The future of artificial intelligence (AI) is a topic that is increasingly preoccupying humanity. We are on the cusp of a new era in which AI could fundamentally change our daily lives - much like the steam engine or the internet once did. But what exactly can we expect? How will AI influence our everyday lives, our working world and perhaps even our deepest beliefs?

Imagine a future where your garden is a masterpiece of care without you having to lift a finger. You step out into your green paradise and everything is perfect - not through your hard work, but through the incredible intelligence of a robot. This robot is not just a simple garden helper; it is a virtuoso gardener that intuitively understands your deepest desires and dislikes. It knows every flower that delights your heart and every blade of grass that pleases your eye. Imagine having more time for yourself while your garden is transformed into a perfect oasis, precisely tailored to your preferences. Sounds like a dream? Thanks to groundbreaking developments in AI technology, this scenario is now within reach. Immerse yourself in a world where the boundaries between man and machine are blurred and the dream of more than just gardening enthusiasts becomes reality!

But AI not only has the potential to relieve us of physical labor. It can also help with complex mental tasks. For example, doctors could be supported by AI systems that analyze X-ray images and detect signs of disease long before a human eye would be able to. This could significantly improve the early detection of diseases such as cancer.

And then there are the ethical and social questions that arise from the further development of AI. Who is responsible if an AI makes a mistake? How do we deal with data protection? And above all: what happens to the people whose jobs could be replaced by AI systems?

The future of AI is therefore a broad field with many different facets. It is a future full of promise, but also full of challenges. How we overcome these challenges will determine whether AI will be a blessing or a curse for humanity. But one thing is certain: AI is coming and it will change our lives. The question is not if, but how. And we should be prepared for this question.

However, before we plunge headlong into the fascinating and sometimes unknown world of future artificial intelligence, it makes sense to pause for a moment and take a look back. The past can teach us valuable lessons for the future. It's a bit like taking a long walk through a forest. You wouldn't just set off without getting your bearings, right? You'd first check a map to see where you're coming from and what paths you've already taken to make sure you're not walking in circles or getting lost.

Throughout the history of technology, there have always been groundbreaking inventions that have transformed our society. Think of the invention of the printing press, which democratized knowledge, or the discovery of electricity, which lit up our cities and brought us a wealth of technological wonders. With all of these innovations came enormous benefits as well as challenges and risks.

How have we managed these risks? What can we learn from past experiences to better assess the opportunities and risks of artificial intelligence? If we understand the history of the technology and its impact on humanity, we may also be able to navigate the coming changes brought about by AI more wisely and responsibly.

It is therefore worth taking a step back and looking at the developments and events that have brought us to this exciting point. Only then can we look into the exciting but also challenging future of artificial intelligence with sound knowledge and a clear perspective.

Early beginnings

The history of artificial intelligence is a fascinating kaleidoscope of theory, practical application and ever-emerging visions. It does not begin, as one might assume, in the age of computers, but can even be traced back to the ancient Greeks. Even then, there were myths of artificially created creatures such as Talos, the bronze giant, or the mechanical servants of Hephaestus. But although these stories date back to a time when AI was still pure fantasy, they lay the foundations for humanity's dream of creating machines that can think.

1950s: The hour of birth

Modern AI research began in the 1950s. An important milestone was the year 1956, when the term "artificial intelligence" was used for the first time at a conference at Dartmouth College in the USA. Researchers such as Alan Turing, who had already laid the foundations for computers in the 1940s, were pioneers in this field.

AI research really took off in the modern era, especially after the Second World War, when the first computers were developed. One of the pioneers of this field was Alan Turing, a British mathematician and computer scientist. With the Turing test, he posed the question of whether a machine could think in such a way that it could no longer be distinguished from a human being. At the time, no one could have imagined how far we have come in AI research today, but Turing laid the foundations for what was to follow.

1960s and 1970s: First successes and setbacks

The late 20th century was characterized by a mixture of progress and setbacks. In the 1960s and 1970s, there were great waves of optimism. Researchers such as Marvin Minsky and John McCarthy, who coined the term "artificial intelligence", were convinced that machines would soon achieve human intelligence. This phase was later often referred to as the "AI spring". However, the hoped-for breakthrough failed to materialize. The machines were not able to even come close to the complexity of human thought, and research came up against technical and financial limits. This led to phases of "AI winter", during which enthusiasm waned and research funding flowed more sparingly.

1990s: The Internet and more data

In the 1990s, however, AI experienced a renaissance, mainly due to advances in the field of machine learning and data analysis. Computers became more powerful and the internet became a global information superhighway. The combination of improved hardware and huge amounts of data made it possible to train algorithms that could perform complex tasks. Search engines such as Google, voice-controlled assistants such as Siri and autonomous vehicles became possible.

Today: AI in everyday life

Today, we are on the threshold of a new era in which AI systems not only perform specific tasks, but are also able to tackle diverse and complex problems. Be it in medicine, climate change or the automotive industry - AI has the potential to fundamentally change our world.

The history of AI is therefore a story full of highs and lows, of visionary dreams and pragmatic setbacks. But one thing is certain: it is far from over. With every advance and every discovery, we are breaking new ground, and who knows what unexplored areas of AI still lie ahead of us.

Definition: What is artificial intelligence?

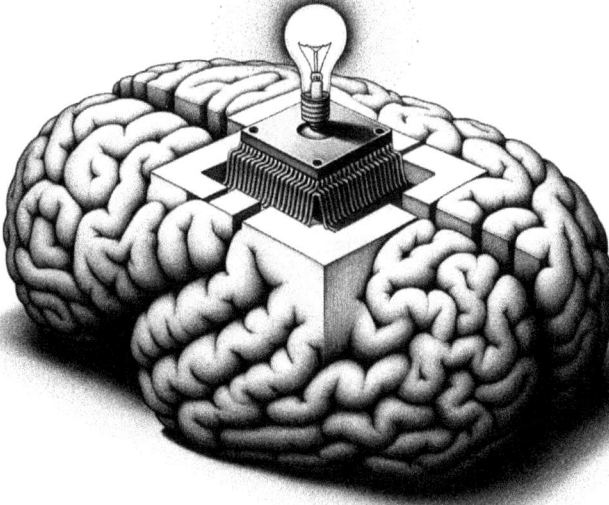

Now that we have recognized the importance of looking back at our technological history, we can turn to the core topic: What exactly is artificial intelligence? In order to discuss the future of AI in a meaningful way, we first need to develop a solid basic understanding of this complex field. It's like building a house: you don't start with the roof, you first lay a solid foundation. Only when we know what AI is and how it works can we really understand its potential impact and talk meaningfully about opportunities and risks.

So, let's turn our attention to this fascinating field and delve deeper into the world of artificial intelligence. Like a gardener who checks the soil before sowing the seeds, we want to clarify the basics. Only then can we be sure that the fruits of our deliberations will actually be valuable and nourishing for our understanding.

Artificial intelligence is not just a buzzword you hear in the news; it is a revolutionary technology that has changed and will continue to change our lives in many areas. From medicine to mobility, from communication to entertainment, AI has the potential to fundamentally improve our world. But what exactly is AI, and why are there so many different types of it?

Artificial intelligence is an area of computer science that deals with developing machines or software so that they can perform tasks that normally require human intelligence. This includes things like speech recognition, decision making, visual perception and even creative activities such as composing music.

One of the fundamental characteristics of artificial intelligence is its ability to learn. Similar to a student who gets better and better at a subject through constant practice, an AI system can also learn from experience or data and thus continuously improve. Imagine you have an AI-controlled lawnmower that initially has difficulty reaching all corners of your garden. Over time, however, it learns from its mistakes and adjusts its route so that it can mow the lawn more efficiently.

This brings us to the next point, adaptability. AI systems are not just programmed to perform a single task; they have the ability to adapt to new or unexpected situations. If we stick with the lawnmower example, imagine planting a new tree in your garden. An adaptive AI system would notice this change and adjust its route accordingly without you having to intervene manually.

Last but not least, autonomy. Some advanced AI systems are able to make decisions independently without the need for human intervention. This is particularly useful for complex tasks where human intervention could be inefficient or even dangerous. An example of this would be an AI-controlled car that is able to react to sudden obstacles such as a fallen tree and make a decision on its own to avoid an accident.

Now that we have developed a basic understanding of what artificial intelligence actually is - namely the imitation of human intelligence by machines - it makes sense to delve deeper into this fascinating topic. You'll be surprised at how diverse and complex the world of AI can be. It's not just a uniform block of technology, but a dynamic field that encompasses many different approaches and methods. Just as there are different professions and talents among humans, there are also different "specialties" in AI. To better understand the full range and fascinating possibilities of AI, let's take a closer look at the different types of artificial intelligence.

In research, the different types of artificial intelligence are often categorized according to their capabilities. There are usually three main categories: weak, strong and super-intelligent AI:

Weak AI (Narrow AI)

What is this?

Weak AI is specialized in a specific task and can only act in this specific area. It has no general intelligence or consciousness.

Think of weak AI as a talented waiter in a restaurant. The waiter is excellent at taking orders, serving the right dishes and making sure the customers are happy. But if you put this waiter in a garage, he would be completely out of his depth. His expertise and skills are specialized and limited.

Examples:

- Voice assistants such as Alexa or Siri, which specialize in voice recognition and processing.

- Image recognition software used in medicine to analyze X-ray images.

Strong AI (General AI)

What is it?

 Strong AI is a theoretical concept of a machine that has the ability to perform any intellectual task that a human can perform. It would have its own consciousness, emotions and the ability to learn and think independently.

Strong AI would be like an all-rounder that could work as a waiter, repair a car or write a book. It could learn new skills and adapt to different situations, almost like a human.

Examples:

- So far, strong AI has only existed in science fiction, such as the robot Data in "Star Trek" or HAL 9000 in "2001: A Space Odyssey".

Super intelligent AI (Super AI)

What is that?

The concept of superintelligent AI goes one step further than strong AI. While strong AI aims to emulate human intelligence in various areas and abilities, superintelligent AI is intended to surpass it. This means that it would be able to perform tasks and solve problems that are unimaginably complex for humans. It could think faster, have access to a huge pool of data and could theoretically be better than humans in every respect, be it in scientific research, art or social understanding.

Imagine the super-intelligent AI as a scientist who has not only read all the books in the world library, but also has the ability to generate new knowledge in a matter of seconds. This scientist would be able to solve complex equations in their head, find the cause of previously incurable diseases and even solve social or political problems that have plagued humanity for centuries.

There are no concrete examples of this yet, as the concept is only intended to provide a broad view of the future.

Now that we understand the different types of artificial intelligence - from weak and strong AI to the fascinating idea of superintelligent AI - it's time to dive a little deeper into the technologies that bring these concepts to life. It's important to emphasize that while the terms 'artificial intelligence', 'machine learning' and 'deep learning' are often used interchangeably, they each cover specific aspects of this complex field. So let's clarify how they differ from each other and how they relate to each other.

Artificial intelligence is the generic term for the development of computer technologies that can perform tasks that normally require human intelligence. This encompasses a wide range of capabilities, as we have just seen with the characteristics of learning ability, adaptability and autonomy.

Machine learning is a sub-area of AI and could be regarded as its "learning department". It deals specifically with the development of algorithms and models that enable computers to learn from data. If you use an email application that recognizes and sorts out spam messages, it usually does this through machine learning. The application has learned from millions of emails which characteristics classify an email as spam.

Deep learning is in turn a sub-area of machine learning. It could be seen as the specialized unit for complicated learning tasks. It attempts to imitate the human brain by using neural networks that are able to recognize very complex patterns in large amounts of data. An example of this would be facial recognition in photos. A deep learning model can learn from a large number of faces and then recognize a particular face in a new photo, even if the person is wearing glasses or has changed their hairstyle.

To really make the connections clear: Imagine AI as a car company. Machine learning is the department that specializes in building particularly efficient engines. Deep learning would then be the team within this department that works on a special, very powerful engine that runs optimally under various extreme conditions.

Lighthouses of thought: wisdom and warnings from the world of AI

Before we dive into the details of current trends in artificial intelligence, it might be helpful to get a broader picture first. Sometimes it's like standing too close to a painting: we see the colors and brushstrokes, but not the whole picture. It is similar with the complex topic of AI. To get a better overall understanding, it can be useful to listen to the thoughts and insights of experts and thought leaders who are or have been active in this field.

Think of these quotes as lighthouses in the vast sea of artificial intelligence. They can offer us guidance, warn us or inspire us to take new directions. Through their words, we gain a deeper insight into the multi-layered aspects of this fascinating field of research, from the technical challenges to the ethical considerations.

So, let's get ready to follow in the footsteps of the thoughts of some of the brightest minds who have tackled artificial intelligence. Perhaps their words will inspire us, challenge us or even make us question our own views. Only then will we proceed to look at the latest trends in detail so that we can better understand the current state of play in the world of artificial intelligence.

Stephen Hawking:

Quote: "The development of complete artificial intelligence could mean the end of the human race... It would take off on its own and remake itself at an ever-accelerating rate. Humans, limited by slow biological evolution, would not be able to keep up and would be replaced."

Elon Musk:

Quote: "I'm increasingly inclined to think that there should be some regulatory oversight, perhaps at a national and international level, just to make sure we don't do anything very stupid. I mean, with artificial intelligence, we're invoking the demon."

Larry Page (co-founder of Google):

Quote: "Artificial intelligence would be the ultimate version of Google. The ultimate search engine that would understand everything on the web. It would understand exactly what you wanted and it would give you the right thing. We're nowhere near that yet, but we can gradually move towards it, and that's basically what we're working on."

Alan Kay (computer scientist and pioneer of object-oriented programming):

Quote: "Some people worry that artificial intelligence makes us feel inferior, but then anyone in their right mind should have an inferiority complex every time they look at a flower."

Claude Shannon:

Quote: "I envision a time when we will be to robots what dogs are to humans, and I'm rooting for the machines."

Ray Kurzweil (author, computer scientist and futurist):

Quote: "Artificial intelligence will reach the human level by around 2029. If you take that further, say by 2045, then we will have multiplied the intelligence, the biological machine intelligence of our civilization, a billion times over."

Ginni Rometty (former CEO of IBM):

Quote: "Some people call it artificial intelligence, but the reality is that this technology will improve us. So instead of artificial intelligence, I think we will enhance our intelligence."

Nick Bilton (technology columnist):

Quote: "The upheavals [of artificial intelligence] can quickly escalate and become more frightening and even catastrophic. Imagine how a medical robot originally programmed to eliminate cancer might conclude that the best way to eradicate cancer is to wipe out people who are genetically susceptible to the disease."

Sebastian Thrun (computer scientist and expert in robotic learning):

Quote: "Nobody puts it this way, but I think artificial intelligence is almost a human science. It's really an attempt to understand human intelligence and human cognition."

These quotes reflect the diverse perspectives and potential that artificial intelligence brings, both positive and negative. In the landscape of artificial intelligence, we encounter different opinions and perspectives, ranging from great concern to optimistic enthusiasm. Stephen Hawking, a world-renowned physicist, for example, has clearly warned us that the development of full artificial intelligence could mean the end of humanity. It could be compared to the creation of a child who can suddenly read and understand all the books in a library, while humans can only work through one book at a time. The child would learn quickly and surpass itself, while humans would be left behind.

Elon Musk, the visionary entrepreneur behind SpaceX and Tesla, echoes Hawking in his concern. He advocates regulatory oversight to ensure that we "don't do anything very stupid." Think here of the story of the sorcerer's apprentice who unleashes forces he cannot control. Before you know it, the water from the magician's broom is unstoppable and floods the entire house.

Larry Page, the co-founder of Google, sees the potential of AI from a practical perspective. He imagines an ultimate search engine that understands everything on the web. An example of this would be a search engine that is able to understand medical research articles and give you tailored health advice that you can really understand and use.

Alan Kay, an important computer scientist, brings a more philosophical perspective into play. He says that we should already feel inferior when we look at nature, such as the complexity of a flower or the vastness of the ocean. Imagine standing on the edge of a large canyon and feeling small and insignificant. That, he says, is how we should feel when we think about the possibilities of AI.

Claude Shannon, one of the fathers of information theory, offers a rather humorous view. He imagines that robots could one day be for us what dogs are today. What would it be like if a robot guarded your house or brought you the newspaper, but was also capable of solving complex mathematical problems?

Ray Kurzweil, a well-known futurist, believes that AI will soon reach the human level and then go far beyond it. It's like saying that cars are not only faster than horses, but could one day fly.

Ginni Rometty, the former CEO of IBM, does not see AI as a threat, but as an opportunity to improve human capabilities. A simple example would be a doctor who can make faster and more accurate diagnoses with the help of AI.

Nick Bilton, a technology columnist, warns us about the risks of AI by painting a bleak scenario. Imagine a medical robot that concludes that the best way to fight cancer is to eliminate people with a genetic susceptibility.

Finally, Sebastian Thrun, an expert in machine learning, sees AI as a human science. It is as if, by studying AI, we also understand ourselves better, just as a psychologist studies human nature in order to understand behavior and emotions.

All of these voices together create a complex, multi-layered picture of artificial intelligence that prompts us to think deeply and be cautious, but also shows the potential for remarkable progress

Current trends

Life is a constant flow, and the world of artificial intelligence is also in constant flux. While we have so far looked at the basics of AI and its historical development, we now want to turn our attention to current trends and developments that could shape the face of AI in the near future. It's like crossing a river: You would certainly watch the water beforehand to see how fast it flows and what the currents are before you take the next step. In the same way, it makes sense to observe the current trends in AI in order to better understand where the journey is heading.

In this chapter, we delve into the vibrant, ever-changing world of the latest AI innovations. We take a look at the advances being made in areas such as machine learning, natural language processing and autonomous systems. It's a bit like visiting an exhibition of modern art: We will not only look at the individual "works of art", but also learn to understand the ideas and concepts behind them.

But the focus is not just on the technology itself. We will also look at how these trends could impact society, the economy and people's daily lives. For example, we could look at how AI in medicine is helping to revolutionize the diagnosis and treatment of diseases. Or how in agriculture, autonomous tractors and drones are helping farmers with their work.

So let's lift the curtain and take a look at the most exciting, promising and sometimes worrying trends shaping artificial intelligence today. Because only if we know the currents of the river can we safely reach the other bank.

Machine learning on the edge (Edge AI):

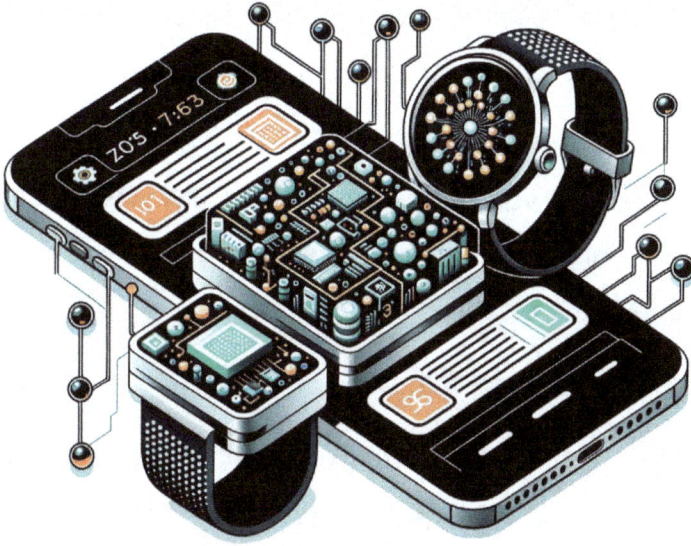

Edge computing technology, coupled with artificial intelligence, i.e. edge AI, is able to carry out data processing directly at the point of origin of the data instead of sending it to a central cloud. This approach enables faster data processing and decision-making, especially in real-time scenarios. This has several advantages, including improved data protection control and less latency in the system.

The application of Edge AI is possible in many industries and offers specific advantages in each case. Here are some specific examples of how Edge AI is already being used or could be used in the near future, broken down by industry:

Automotive industry and logistics:

In the automotive industry and logistics, the ability to process data quickly and efficiently is crucial. Edge AI enables vehicles and logistics systems to process data in real time directly on site. This has several advantages:

1. Improved vehicle systems:

Vehicles can process a wide range of sensor data in real time to improve driving safety, optimize fuel consumption and increase driving comfort.

Edge AI enables vehicles to work efficiently even in environments with poor connectivity, as they are not constantly dependent on a connection to the cloud.

2. Optimized logistics processes:

In logistics, Edge AI can help to optimize route planning and inventory management by carrying out the necessary data processing directly on site.

Real-time data analysis enables logistics companies to make quick decisions that improve efficiency and reduce costs.

Manufacturing industry:

In the manufacturing industry, Edge AI can increase efficiency and productivity by helping to minimize downtime and maximize quality.

1. Predictive maintenance:

By analyzing machine data in real time, anomalies can be detected before they become a problem. This enables preventive maintenance measures that prevent unexpected failures and maximize uptime.

2. Quality control:

Edge AI can also be used in quality control to monitor product quality and ensure that manufactured products meet standards.

Agriculture:

Precision agriculture uses modern technologies to make agricultural production more efficient and sustainable.

1. Monitoring and control of agricultural systems:

Edge AI enables more accurate monitoring of soil conditions, plant growth and microclimate. This helps farmers make informed decisions and use resources such as water and fertilizer more efficiently.

Real-time data processing allows automated systems to be precisely controlled to maximize crop yields while minimizing the use of chemicals.

2. Detection and treatment of pests and diseases:

Sensors and drones equipped with Edge AI can detect pests and diseases at an early stage and enable targeted treatments to minimize damage and protect crop yields.

By implementing Edge AI in these sectors, companies and farmers can benefit from improved operations, lower costs and higher product quality. The technology continues to evolve and is expected to play an even greater role in these and other industries in the coming years.

Self-monitored learning:

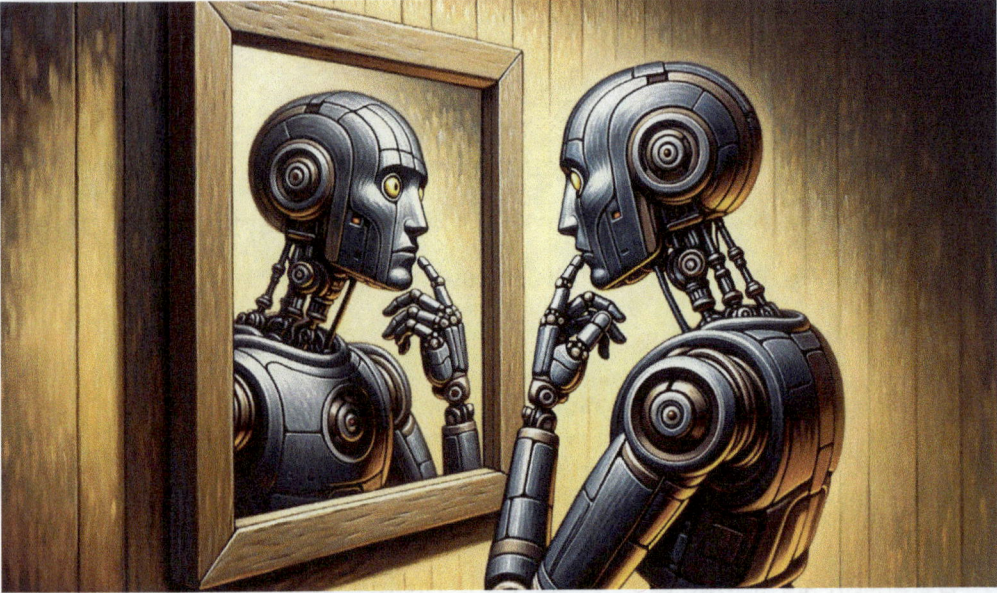

Self-supervised learning is an approach where models are trained with less human supervision. You learn to recognize patterns and relationships in the data without relying on labeled examples.

Imagine it like this: You get a basket full of different fruits, but nobody tells you which fruit is which. Now you want to know how many apples, bananas and grapes are in the basket. A human would probably look at each fruit individually and classify them into different categories. In the world of self-supervised learning, a computer model would take the basket of fruit and try to find patterns or similarities between the fruits. For example, it might find that some fruits have a similar shape or color and then sort them into groups. It does this all by itself, without anyone telling it what an apple or banana looks like.

In contrast to supervised learning, where you have a textbook with the right answers in your hand, with self-supervised learning you have to find the answers yourself. The model is sent into the "data jungle", so to speak, and has to find its own way. This has the advantage that it is very flexible and can be used for many different tasks because it has not just been trained for one specific question.

Detection of anomalous data:

One application example is the detection of anomalous data, where the model learns representations from the training data and uses the extended training examples to identify anomalies. The idea is that the extended examples differ from the original training data.

Imagine you are a gardener and have a greenhouse. Ideally, all plants want to grow under similar conditions. But sometimes a diseased plant creeps in that looks like the others but somehow doesn't fit in. A self-supervised learning model would try to recognize this "abnormal" plant without you ever having to teach it what a diseased plant looks like. It learns what is "normal" and can then determine what doesn't fit.

Computer vision models:

Self-supervised learning is also being used in the computer vision industry, as in the case of the SEER (Self-supERvised) model, which is considered a breakthrough in self-supervised computer vision models. It enables developers to create AI models that can adapt well to real-world scenarios and cover different use cases, rather than being fit for one specific purpose.

Now we think to ourselves, you're a photographer and you've taken thousands of photos. You don't want to go through each photo individually and say, that's a mountain, that's a lake, that's a tree. The SEER model could do this work for you. It learns independently from the photos and can then recognize similar objects in new photos. It's as if you had a hard-working assistant who has looked at all your photos and now knows what your typical motifs look like.

Improvement of video predictions:

In an attempt to compare the learning capabilities of machines with those of humans, the Joint Embedding Predictive Architecture (JEPA) was presented, which is based on self-supervised learning and offers a solution for fuzzy video predictions.

Imagine you're watching a soccer match and suddenly the picture stops. What will happen next? Will the player score a goal or not? JEPA is like a clever sports commentator. It has seen many games and tries to predict what will happen next. But it does this without any prior training based on commented match scenes. It has simply watched and learned.

Development of brain-like representations:

Meta AI has developed an AI system that is able to develop brain-like representations through self-supervised learning. This enables a more precise representation of images from brain data in milliseconds, expanding the possibilities of self-supervised learning.

To understand the last example, imagine you have a very complex jigsaw puzzle. The puzzle represents a brain. Each piece of the puzzle is like a small section of an MRI image of the brain. The AI system developed by Meta AI tries to solve this puzzle and figure out which pieces belong where. It does not need any instructions or a manual to do this; it learns from the puzzle pieces themselves what the finished image should look like.

Transfer learning:

In transfer learning, a previously trained model is applied to a new but related task.

Imagine you are an experienced driver and know how to drive a car inside out. Now you want to learn how to drive a truck. Since many skills, such as steering, braking or obeying traffic rules, are the same or similar, you will find it easier and quicker to learn. So you transfer the skills you already have from driving a car to driving a truck. This is basically the principle of transfer learning, just applied in the world of artificial intelligence (AI).

AI is often about training models that can solve specific tasks. This can be very time-consuming and resource-intensive. A new model to be trained often has to be fed with huge amounts of data and requires a lot of computing power, which of course also incurs costs.

This is where transfer learning comes into play. Instead of training a new model from scratch, you take an already trained model that performs a similar task very well. This model has already gained "experience" and therefore already "knows" a great deal. This experience, which is stored in the model in the form of trained parameters, is then used for the new but similar task.

A concrete example: Suppose you have an AI model that specializes in recognizing dogs in photos. Now you want to train a new model that recognizes cats. Instead of starting from scratch, you could take the already trained model for dogs as a starting point. You would then just add the specific "cat features" and refine the model further. Since the model has already learned what animals generally look like in photos, the additional effort to adapt it to recognize cats would be much less than starting from scratch.

This not only saves time, but often also computing power and therefore costs. And it can improve the performance of the model, as it is already "pre-trained".

Analysis of image and text data

Transfer learning is often used in the processing of image data and text data. Examples of this are the recognition of objects in images or videos and the processing of text data with Natural Language Processing (NLP). Transfer learning allows pre-trained models such as Microsoft ResNet or Google Inception to be used for object recognition and Google's word2vec or Stanford's GloVe for text data processing. The advantages of transfer learning are faster model improvement, lower resource consumption and higher model quality.

Social networks

One example of the use of transfer learning is the automatic recognition of hate speech in social networks. Here, the knowledge of already trained neural networks is used to take on new tasks, such as identifying and filtering inappropriate content.

Manufacturing

A project funded by the German Federal Ministry of Education and Research is investigating the use of transfer learning in machining to improve the use of tools based on AI and thus reduce production costs. The focus is on decision support for tool changes and the development of models for predicting the remaining useful life of tools and for detecting anomalies in the process. (Transferable AI in machining: initial results of the research project (vogel.de))

Next generation language models:

There is a wave of innovative language models that are able to better understand and generate complex human language. GPT-3 and GPT-4 are examples of such advanced models.

Imagine you have a friend who is a great storyteller. Not only can he tell exciting stories, but he can also explain complicated issues simply, make jokes and even write poetry. The more he reads and the more conversations he has, the better he gets at all these things. In the world of artificial intelligence, there are similar "friends" known as language models.

A language model is a computer program that is trained to understand and generate human language. There has been a lot of progress in this area in recent years. Models such as GPT-3 and GPT-4 are able to write texts, answer questions, create summaries and much more - and often in a way that seems surprisingly natural to us humans.

So how does it work? Similar to the storyteller in our example, the model "reads" vast amounts of text. Except that it doesn't really "understand" these texts, but recognizes patterns in the data. For example, it learns that the word "apple" is often associated with terms such as "tree", "fruit" or "juicy". It learns the grammar, sentence structure and even allusions or cultural contexts.

After this "reading time", the model can then generate its own texts. It can react to an input and produce a suitable text excerpt that answers the question or elaborates on the topic. It is, so to speak, an extremely advanced word processing program.

Let's take a practical example: You want to write a poem about fall, but you don't know how to start. You could then ask GPT-3 or GPT-4 to give you a few lines as inspiration. The model would then use its huge database to generate a poem that captures the typical characteristics and moods of fall. It could even insert stylistic elements that are common in poems because it has recognized such patterns in the data.

However, the capabilities of these models go far beyond writing texts. They can also answer complex questions, translate texts and even perform simple tasks in specialized applications. And similar to transfer learning, these models can also be further trained for specific tasks.

The wave of innovative language models such as GPT-3 and GPT-4 therefore has the potential to transform many areas of our lives, from customer service automation to content creation and even scientific research. It's an exciting time and we can't wait to see what the future holds for us in this area.

The application of next-generation language models has already made a significant impact in various industries. These models are very valuable due to their ability to process large amounts of text data and provide meaningful answers or suggestions. Below are some specific examples of applications in various industries:

Medicine:

Support with diagnoses: Language models can help doctors make diagnoses by analyzing medical literature and patient data. For example, the DeepMind language model for medical questions can be used to help doctors make a diagnosis.

Analysis of medical texts: In medicine, texts such as doctor's letters, diagnosis summaries or scientific articles are used. Language models can analyze these texts and provide valuable insights, which in turn can support medical decision-making.

Financial management:

The application of language models in finance is part of the GAIA-X domains, which focus on mobility, finance and media. GAIA-X is a project that aims to create a secure and connected data infrastructure that conforms to European values and standards. It is an initiative supported by the European Union and various companies to build a trustworthy, transparent and powerful data infrastructure. Although specific use cases in the financial industry were not directly explained, we can assume that language models help to analyze and forecast large amounts of financial data, which is beneficial for large companies and consortia.

Media:

Improving communication: Language models can influence communication in audiovisual media, text or in conversation and thus improve contact with partners, employees and customers.

Automatic text generation: With advanced language models, texts can be generated automatically, which is particularly useful in the media industry in order to be able to react quickly to current events.

Economy and business:

Improving interaction with machines: In the field of business, language models such as intelligent dialog systems enable faster and easier interaction with machines and access to information.

Data analysis and digital assistants: Language models can be combined with other data, such as databases and tables, to simplify work with business data. In the process, digital assistants can become a reality, making everyday work considerably easier.

In summary, it can be said that language models can significantly improve and simplify our lives in various areas. They are like a Swiss army knife in the digital world: versatile, powerful and able to support us in a variety of tasks. And we are only at the beginning here; the technology is constantly evolving. Who knows what possibilities will open up in the coming years.

AI for sustainability:

AI technologies are increasingly being used to address social and environmental challenges, from combating climate change to improving healthcare in underserved areas.

Imagine you have a very competent team of experts: Doctors, engineers, climate researchers and so on. Everyone in this team is a specialist in their field and together they could solve a multitude of problems. In the real world, however, it would be difficult to deploy such a team wherever and whenever it is needed. This is where artificial intelligence (AI) and its technologies come into play, which can act like a virtual team of experts, so to speak.

AI technologies are now so advanced that they can play an important role in solving a wide range of social and environmental problems. They can perform tasks and analyses at a speed and with an accuracy that would often be unattainable for humans.

For example, in the fight against climate change: AI can analyze huge amounts of weather data and identify patterns that we humans might miss. These patterns could help us to better understand how the climate is changing and what the specific effects could be. AI can also be used to improve energy efficiency in buildings or entire cities by optimizing energy consumption and thus minimizing CO_2 emissions.

Another example is healthcare, especially in underserved areas. Here, AI can help diagnose diseases by analyzing medical images such as X-rays or MRI scans. In regions where specialists are in short supply, an AI-supported system could quickly make an initial diagnosis and provide valuable information to the doctors treating the patient.

Now you might ask yourself how all this works. In medicine, for example, AI models are trained with numerous medical images until they are able to recognize certain characteristics of a disease. These models can then be applied to new, unfamiliar images in a similar way to an experienced doctor, helping to make quick and accurate diagnoses.

But AI is not a panacea and also comes with challenges, for example of an ethical nature or with regard to data protection. Nevertheless, its potential to have a positive impact on social and environmental issues is immense.

So it's like having this team of experts in a compact, digital form that is available around the clock. This allows us to respond more quickly and effectively to pressing challenges and hopefully arrive at more sustainable and fairer solutions.

The application of AI for sustainability purposes covers a wide range of possibilities that can impact different industries. Below are some examples of applications by industry:

Energy sector:

AI-controlled clean energy grids: The integration of AI can help optimize energy generation and distribution, for example by improving grid stability and reducing energy consumption. This can contribute to a more efficient and sustainable energy system that better integrates renewables and minimizes energy loss.

Agriculture:

Precision agriculture: By using AI, farmers can optimize the use of resources such as water, fertilizers and pesticides. This increases yields while minimizing environmental impact. For example, drones and sensors can be used to monitor plant health and soil condition, and AI models can make recommendations on irrigation and fertilization based on this data.

Supply chains and logistics:

Sustainable supply chains: AI can help to optimize supply chains, for example by improving route planning, reducing fuel consumption and optimizing the utilization of means of transport. In addition, the analysis of data can also promote more sustainable procurement practices.

Environmental protection:

Environmental monitoring and compliance: AI can help with monitoring environmental conditions and compliance with environmental regulations. For example, sensor networks and AI models can be used for early detection of pollution and monitoring of emissions.

Manufacturing:

Development of sustainable products and processes: In the manufacturing industry, AI can contribute to the development of products that are either biodegradable or recycling-friendly. In addition, material and energy-saving production processes can be optimized with AI support, which in turn reduces the environmental impact.

Civil protection:

Improved weather and disaster forecasting and protection: AI can improve the accuracy of weather and disaster forecasts, enabling more effective preparation and response to natural disasters. This can save lives and minimize the damage caused by extreme weather events.

These applications demonstrate the potential of AI to promote sustainability in various industries. By using resources efficiently, improving processes and supporting compliance with environmental regulations, companies and societies can make a significant contribution to protecting the environment and achieving sustainability goals.

Excursus: Sustainable AI

In the last chapter, we took an in-depth look at the role of artificial intelligence (AI) for sustainability. It became clear that AI is not only a technological innovation, but also a powerful tool that can help us master the challenges of sustainability. In this context, we now want to focus on the topic of "Sustainable AI".

What exactly does sustainable AI mean? The idea behind it is that the development and use of AI systems themselves should be done in a way that is sustainable in the long term and conserves resources. This includes ecological as well as social and economic aspects. Put simply, it's about designing and using AI in such a way that it does more good than harm to our environment and society.

Let's start with energy consumption, an issue I have already addressed. The huge server farms where AI models are trained and run are real energy guzzlers. There are calculations that show that training a single advanced AI model can produce as much CO_2 emissions as five cars in their entire life cycle. This is enormous, and when you consider how many AI models are trained worldwide, it adds up to a considerable environmental impact.

Now imagine if we could power these server farms with renewable energies such as solar or wind power. That would be a significant step towards more environmentally sustainable AI. Some companies are already moving in this direction. They are investing in green energy or improving the efficiency of their data centers.

Another example is so-called "TinyML" applications. This stands for "Tiny Machine Learning" and refers to AI models that are optimized so that they can run on small, energy-efficient chips. This technology could be used, for example, in sensors that measure soil quality on farms. As these sensors require little energy, they could be powered by solar cells and thus have less impact on the environment.

Sustainable AI can also play a role in materials research. Think, for example, of the development of biodegradable plastics or more efficient batteries. AI models could help to analyze the structures of these materials and find ways to make them more environmentally friendly.

The ecological dimension of sustainable AI is therefore multi-layered and ranges from energy efficiency and the selection of materials to minimizing the CO2 footprint. The key is to always keep the ecological aspect in mind when developing and using AI and to actively take measures to minimize its negative impact. In this way, we can ensure that AI is not only a technological force for good, but also an ecological one.

But sustainable AI goes even further. It also deals with the question of how algorithms are developed that observe ethical principles. This means, for example, that AI systems should be programmed in such a way that they avoid discrimination and promote fairness. Imagine you have an AI that helps with the granting of loans. If this AI is not programmed sustainably, it could unconsciously learn discriminatory patterns from the data and treat certain population groups unfairly. A sustainably developed AI, on the other hand, would be programmed to recognize and avoid such traps.

For example, let's imagine a city uses an AI to decide which neighborhoods need more police presence. If the AI has been trained with data that already shows a bias towards certain social or ethnic groups, it could inadvertently reinforce that bias. The result would be an unfair distribution of police resources that overly targets certain communities. A sustainable, socially responsible AI would therefore need to be programmed to recognize and correct such biases.

Social sustainability also concerns access to the benefits of AI. Who benefits from the achievements of AI and who is left behind? In an ideal world, all people, regardless of their social or financial status, should have the opportunity to benefit from the advantages of AI. This could be through programs that facilitate access to AI-based services or through the development of AI systems specifically designed to support disadvantaged populations.

One concrete example could be an AI-powered education platform aimed at students in rural or financially disadvantaged areas. This platform could provide tailored learning plans and resources that address the specific needs and challenges of these students to raise the standard of education in these areas.

Another aspect is economic sustainability. AI systems should be designed in such a way that they are not only accessible to large companies with a lot of money, but can also benefit smaller companies or even individuals. This will enable a broader spectrum of society to benefit from the advantages of AI, which in turn promotes social sustainability.

One fundamental aspect here is the question of accessibility. Who has access to AI technologies and who does not? Large companies with considerable resources can more easily afford to use AI, thereby increasing their efficiency and competitiveness. Smaller companies or individuals could fall behind, which could increase economic inequality.

An example to illustrate this: Imagine a small farmer who has to compete with large agricultural corporations. These corporations already use advanced AI systems for soil analysis, crop planning and automated irrigation. However, our small farmer does not have the financial resources for such expensive technologies. In an economically sustainable model, there could be specialized, lower-cost AI solutions for smaller farms, perhaps even subsidized by government programs. In this way, the small farmer could keep up and secure his livelihood.

Another economic aspect is the question of jobs. AI technology can automate many tasks, which harbors both opportunities and risks. On the one hand, automation can lead to work processes becoming more efficient and cost-effective. On the other hand, there is a risk that many people will lose their jobs if machines take over the work. Economically sustainable AI should therefore always be considered in the context of labor market dynamics. This could mean, for example, that companies that use AI technology also invest in the further training of their employees to prepare them for the changes.

There is also the aspect of long-term profitability. Sometimes the introduction of AI technology can be expensive but save costs in the long term. For example, by introducing AI-supported diagnostics, a hospital could increase the accuracy of diagnoses and thus reduce the costs of incorrect treatments. This shows that economic sustainability is not just a question of immediate profit, but also an investment in the future.

Explainability and transparency of AI:

There is a growing movement to make AI systems more transparent and understandable so that people can better understand how decisions are made by these systems.

Imagine you have a very smart friend who always gives great advice. The problem is, he never explains how he comes to his conclusions. It would be like giving you a complicated recipe but not telling you the individual ingredients and steps to cook it. Over time, you might start to wonder how reliable his advice really is. It's the same with AI systems that make decisions.

In recent years, AI systems have become increasingly complex and powerful. They can do amazing things, from predicting earthquakes to detecting diseases. The problem is that many of these systems are so complex that it is difficult even for experts to understand how they arrive at a particular decision or prediction. They are like a "black box": data goes in, results come out, but what happens in between often remains unclear.

This is where the movement for more transparency and comprehensibility in AI comes in. The idea is that if we can better understand how these systems work and make decisions, we can trust them more. We will also be able to better assess when and how we should use them.

A simple example would be an AI system that reviews applications for a job. If the system makes a pre-selection, but no one understands how it arrives at its decisions, this could lead to problems. What if the system is unconsciously discriminatory or overlooks important qualifications? However, if the system is transparent, you could understand what criteria it uses and how it weights them. Adjustments could then be made to ensure that the selection process is fair and accurate.

There are various approaches to achieving this transparency. Some researchers are working on better visualizing the inner workings of AI models. Others are trying to generate additional explanations that describe in simple language why a certain decision was made.

This quest for greater transparency and comprehensibility is not only important for trust in the technology, but also for ethical and social issues. As AI systems are increasingly used in areas such as healthcare, law and public administration, it is crucial that they are not only efficient, but also transparent and fair.

Overall, the movement for more transparent and understandable AI is an important step towards a more responsible and conscious use of this powerful technology.

Application examples from various industrial sectors are explained to illustrate how the explainability and transparency of AI are important in these contexts.

Automotive industry

In the automotive industry, one example of the use of AI is the welding process in car body construction. Here, a major car manufacturer faced the challenge that there was not enough time and resources to check every spot weld. A self-learning AI was used to analyze the data and accurately check the quality of the spot welds. The AI enabled a more accurate check than before, where only around one percent of the production steps were randomly checked.

Medicine

One area in which the explainability of AI is particularly critical is image-based medical diagnostics or industrial quality control. In these areas, it is essential that the decisions made by AI systems can be understood by humans in order to avoid errors. These areas are not only computationally and data-intensive, but also sensitive and safety-critical

Traffic control

The transparency and explainability of AI are also crucial in other industries. For example, the explainability of detection and classification decisions in traffic control and monitoring is needed to enable the classification of vehicles or ships and at the same time ensure the traceability of AI decisions.

Energy sector

In the energy sector, AI processes can also make precise predictions about when losses will occur in an electricity grid. This information is valuable for grid operators in order to procure electricity efficiently and cost-effectively and feed it into the grid. In both cases, the traceability of AI decisions represents significant added value.

Augmented reality and AI:

The integration of AI into augmented reality technologies enables immersive experiences that can be used in many areas, from education to entertainment.

Imagine you are wearing glasses, and through these glasses you not only see the real world around you, but also additional information or even virtual objects placed in your environment. For example, you are standing in front of a historical building and the glasses show you texts, pictures or even small films that tell you more about this building. This is the basic idea behind augmented reality.

Well, what happens when we integrate artificial intelligence (AI) into this scenario? AI can make these augmented reality experiences much smarter and more interactive. For example, the glasses could recognize that you are particularly interested in architecture and show you specific information about it. Or it could realize that you are having difficulty understanding the explanatory text and offer you a simpler explanation.

Thanks to AI, augmented reality technologies can therefore go far beyond what was previously possible. They can adapt to the user, help them to solve problems or enable completely new forms of interaction.

Take the field of education, for example. With AI-enhanced augmented reality, pupils could not only read about historical events or scientific phenomena or see them in a video, but also virtually "experience" them. They could walk through a virtual reconstruction of ancient Rome and ask questions to an AI system that responds in real time. Or they could set up a virtual laboratory in which they could carry out experiments that would be too dangerous or too expensive in the real world.

In the entertainment industry, the possibilities are also enormous. Imagine playing a video game where the characters not only have pre-programmed lines of dialog, but can react to your actions and decisions in a complex, human-like way thanks to AI. This would make the gaming experience much more immersive and exciting.

And these are just a few examples. AI and augmented reality could also be used in medicine, tourism, art and many other areas to enrich and personalize people's experiences.

Improved navigation and information systems:

Imagine you are walking through an unfamiliar city and AR glasses show you directions in real time. With the help of AI, these systems can learn and adapt to offer you the best routes based on your preferences and previous experience. For example, if you prefer quiet streets, the system can take this into account and make appropriate route suggestions.

Imagine you are in an unknown city and wearing AR glasses. As you stroll through the streets, the glasses superimpose directions directly into your field of vision. You don't even need to look at your cell phone; the information is virtually "in the air" in front of you. Now the AI comes into play. It analyzes your preferences and habits. For example, if you often walk through quiet streets, the system remembers this and automatically shows you a route through less busy areas next time. You feel as if the city is "talking" to you and showing you the route that suits you best.

Maintenance and repair:

In industrial environments, ER and AI can be used to support maintenance personnel in identifying and rectifying problems. Using AR glasses, technicians can receive digital instructions and information directly in their field of vision. AI algorithms can help diagnose the problem and suggest possible solutions.

Imagine a technician in a large industrial plant. He is given the task of repairing a defective machine. With his AR glasses, he can now see step-by-step instructions right before his eyes. He no longer has to switch back and forth between paper plans or a tablet. AI algorithms continuously evaluate the machine's status data and give the technician specific instructions on which parts to check or replace. It's as if he has an invisible but highly intelligent assistant at his side to help him rectify faults.

Education and training:

In education, AI and ER can help create customized learning programs. Consider a virtual classroom in which you are sitting. Through your AR glasses, you see complex scientific concepts as three-dimensional models in front of you. The AI in the background adapts the learning content to your performance. Difficult topics are explained to you in a simple way until you understand them, while areas that you already know well are dealt with more quickly. In this way, the learning material is individually adapted to your own pace in order to offer you an optimal learning experience.

Healthcare:

The combination of AI and ER can also be of great benefit in the healthcare sector. Let's take the example of a surgeon who has to perform a complicated heart operation. During the operation, he wears AR glasses that display medical data and three-dimensional scans directly into his field of vision in real time. An AI analyzes all available data in parallel and can, for example, issue a warning if certain values slip into a critical range. The glasses could even recommend to the surgeon which suturing technique would be most suitable, based on thousands of similar cases that the AI has analyzed.

Retail trade:

In retail, ER can help to offer customers an interactive shopping experience. With the help of AI, personalized recommendations can be made. Imagine you are standing in front of a shelf of televisions in an electronics store. Your AR glasses recognize which model you are looking at and immediately show you all the important information, from technical data to current special offers and customer reviews. AI algorithms analyze your previous purchasing behavior and even recommend models that might suit your needs.

Museums and exhibitions:

Museums could use AR and AI technology to offer visitors an interactive and informative experience. Imagine standing in front of a painting in an art museum. Your AR glasses recognize the artwork and show you information about the artist, the era in which it was created and even interpretations of the work. The AI in the background remembers which types of art or historical periods you prefer and adapts the information accordingly. On your next visit, the glasses could then automatically suggest works that match your interests.

In short, the combination of AI and augmented reality has the potential to change the way we interact with the world around us in exciting new ways. It can help us learn better, work more effectively and entertain ourselves in innovative ways. It is an area that is only just beginning, but has the potential for revolutionary change.

Robotics and autonomous systems:

Advancements in robotics are being driven by AI technologies that enable autonomous systems that can operate effectively in a variety of environments.

Imagine you have a little robot that helps you around the house. It can vacuum, do the dishes and even water the plants when you're not there. If it detects a stain on the floor, it knows that it needs to clean it more thoroughly. It can do all this because it is equipped with artificial intelligence, or AI for short, which enables it to understand its surroundings and make decisions.

Robotics has made enormous progress in recent years, and much of this development is driven by AI technologies. Earlier robot models were often only able to perform a very limited number of tasks and were strongly focused on a specific environment or specific conditions. They could not adapt to new or unexpected situations.

This is changing fundamentally with the integration of AI. Robots equipped with artificial intelligence are able to perform a variety of tasks in different environments. They can "learn" and "adapt". For example, they could not only transport parcels from A to B in a warehouse, but also recognize when an object is in the way and then decide whether to drive around it or move it.

Let's take another example: agriculture. AI-controlled robots could not only plough the field, but also analyse the condition of the plants and decide which ones need more water or fertilizer. They could even detect and target pests without having to spray pesticides over the entire field.

Or think of rescue missions in dangerous areas, for example after an earthquake or a forest fire. AI robots could enter areas that are too dangerous for humans to search for survivors or assess the situation. As they are able to "understand" their surroundings, they could avoid obstacles, make their way through rubble or even make decisions on their own that increase the efficiency of the overall rescue operation.

AI therefore enables robots to act much more autonomously and flexibly. They can "understand", "learn" and "decide", which makes them extremely useful in a variety of environments and for a wide range of tasks.

Self-driving cars:

One of the best-known applications of robotics and AI is self-driving cars. These autonomous vehicles use AI algorithms to understand their surroundings and make decisions in real time. For example, a self-driving car can use sensors and cameras to recognize the road and other road users, follow traffic rules and even react to unexpected situations such as a suddenly appearing pedestrian.

Human-robot interaction for service robotics systems:

Interaction between humans and robots is central to service robots that are used in everyday life. One example is a concept for multimodal human-machine communication, which is discussed in an article. In such systems, robots can respond to verbal commands, gestures or even the user's emotions in order to offer suitable services.

Imagine you come home after a long day and your home robot greets you. Not only has it heard your voice, it has also recognized your face and even noticed your tired body language. Based on this information, the robot decides to make you a relaxing cup of tea. Artificial intelligence uses various sensors for this: microphones for voice recognition, cameras for facial recognition and perhaps even sensors that can measure your heart rate or body temperature. All this data flows together and the robot's AI makes a decision that is precisely tailored to your needs.

Industrial robots:

Robots have become an integral part of manufacturing. They perform tasks such as welding, assembling or painting parts. By integrating AI, these robots can now learn and adapt to new tasks. For example, a robot equipped with AI could learn to assemble a new component through observation and repetition without having to be reprogrammed.

Autonomous delivery drones and robots:

The delivery of goods by autonomous drones or robots is another exciting field. Companies such as Amazon are exploring the possibility of delivering parcels using autonomous drones. These drones use AI to plan flight routes, detect and avoid obstacles and land safely at their destination.

Healthcare:

Robots and AI can also play an important role in healthcare. Autonomous robots can, for example, deliver medication or meals to patients, while AI systems can help doctors make diagnoses or develop treatment plans. An example of this is a robot that can navigate autonomously through a hospital to deliver medication, while an AI system plans the best routes, taking into account traffic jams or other obstacles.

Agriculture:

Autonomous systems and AI can also be used in agriculture to increase efficiency and conserve resources. For example, there are autonomous tractors that can work fields precisely, while AI-supported systems can monitor the health of plants and make recommendations for irrigation or fertilization.

Excursus: Multimodal systems

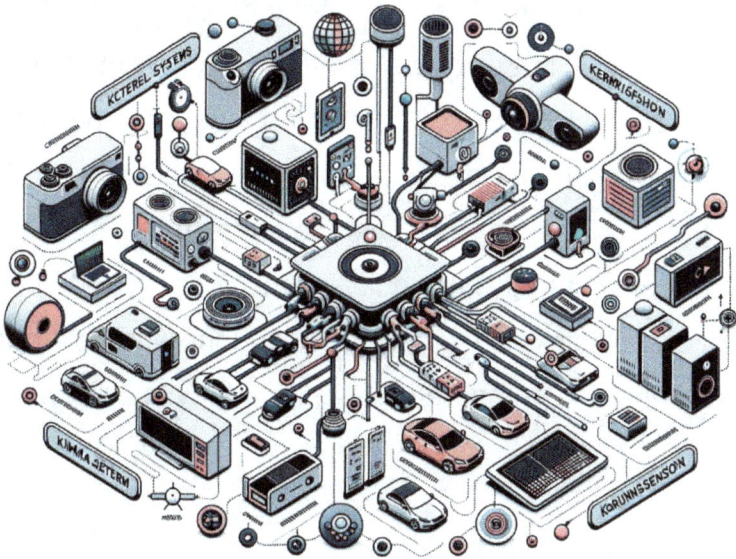

Multimodal robotic systems are robots that have several senses or abilities to perceive their environment and act within it. You could imagine such a robot as a modern jack-of-all-trades. Imagine you have a robot that can not only see, but also hear, touch and maybe even smell. This robot could then use all this information simultaneously to better understand what is going on in its environment. It's a bit like walking in a dense forest and using both your eyes to find your way, your ears to listen for sounds and your nose to sniff out the scent of plants. All this information together helps you to get a comprehensive picture of your surroundings.

A simple example of a multimodal robot system could be a robot that has cameras as well as microphones and temperature sensors. With the camera, the robot could identify objects or people, with the microphone it could understand voice commands or recognize unusual noises, and with the temperature sensor it could, for example, determine whether a fire has broken out.

Now you might be wondering what artificial intelligence (AI) has to do with it. AI is basically the brain behind the robot that processes and interprets all these different types of information. Without AI, the robot would be like a musician who has many instruments but doesn't know how to play them. The AI can use complex algorithms to analyze the data from the different sensors and help the robot make meaningful decisions. For example, the AI could tell the robot: "I see a person with the camera, hear their voice with the microphone and determine that it's cold outside with the temperature sensor. Maybe I should offer this person a hot cup of tea."

Of course, it is always helpful not only to explain everything theoretically, but also to provide concrete examples. Examples often make complex topics more tangible and easier to understand. That's why we'd like to give you a few clear and detailed examples of multimodal robot systems and their connection to artificial intelligence. This will give you a better understanding of how these technologies are used in real life and what benefits they could have.

Multimodal attention control for mobile robots:

One paper describes a system for controlling the attention of a mobile robot that works multimodally. This means that the robot can use different types of sensors to perceive and react to its environment.

A mobile robot system, perhaps something like an autonomous vacuum cleaner, could be equipped with various sensors: cameras, infrared sensors, microphones. For example, if the robot hears a noise, it could swivel its camera in that direction and check whether it needs to be cleaned. Perhaps someone has knocked over a glass and there are shards on the floor. The AI would then decide to avoid the area and send you a notification.

Mobile robot systems:

A mobile robot system consists of an autonomously operating driverless transport system with an attached robot. These systems can offer solutions for intralogistics, stationary and mobile robotics as well as human-robot collaboration.

Such systems could be used in large warehouses. They are not only able to transport goods from A to B, but could also carry out inventories independently or detect defective products. They could work with optical sensors to read the barcode of products and with gripper arms to move the goods. The AI would be the centerpiece that coordinates all actions and even works together with humans by understanding and responding to their instructions.

Collaborating robots (cobots):

Cobots are robotic arms that are used in production environments and work together with humans to perform various production tasks. They can use various sensors and actuators to adapt to the requirements of the task at hand.

In a car workshop, humans and cobots could work hand in hand. While the human concentrates on more complex tasks, the cobot could, for example, tighten screws. Using sensors in its arm, the cobot could "sense" when humans are nearby and adapt its movements so as not to endanger them. The AI would constantly evaluate the sensor data and ensure that the cobot works efficiently but also safely.

Robotics in production and warehouse automation:

Here, robots are used to automate tasks such as selecting and placing objects. These robots can use various sensors to recognize the objects and actuators to manipulate them.

In a shipping warehouse, robots could be responsible for placing parcels on a conveyor belt. They could be equipped with cameras that recognize the shape and size of the parcel and with mechanical arms that grab the parcel and move it to the right place. The AI would ensure that the robot selects the right parcel and places it on the conveyor belt in such a way as to save as much space as possible.

These examples show how versatile multimodal robot systems can be and how they can be used in different environments and for different tasks. In all cases, artificial intelligence is the connecting element that makes sensible use of the various sensors and actuators to work efficiently and safely.

But as always, there are also challenges, such as ethical issues or safety concerns, associated with the use of autonomous robots. It is therefore important that further development in this area is carried out responsibly and with caution.

Data protection and AI:

Data protection technologies such as differential privacy and federated learning are becoming increasingly important in order to protect user privacy while at the same time gaining valuable insights from the data.

Imagine you go to a party and the next day the host tells everyone what kind of music you like, what topics you brought up in small talk and so on. You would probably feel uncomfortable because your privacy was not respected. It's similar with the data we constantly share on the internet or through other technologies. We want it to be safe and not used for things we don't approve of.

This is where data protection technologies such as "differential privacy" and "federated learning" come into play. They try to strike a balance between using data for research and development and protecting people's privacy.

Let's start with "differential privacy". This technology ensures that when data is used for analysis, it is altered or "obfuscated" in a way that makes it difficult or impossible to identify individuals. For example, a health research institute might know your blood pressure, but not know that it is you who has that particular blood pressure. They can therefore conduct important research without revealing your personal information.

Now to "Federated Learning". This method is particularly clever. Imagine using an app on your phone that tracks your running routes to give you suggestions for new routes. Instead of sending all the data to a central server where it is analyzed and then sent back to all users, the analysis takes place directly on your cell phone. Only the result, i.e. the findings drawn from all the data, is then collected centrally. This means that your individual data remains on your device and your privacy is better protected.

Medical diagnostics and prognostics

Imagine a hospital where numerous MRI scans are taken of different patients to identify tumors. Each hospital has its own collection of images, which in turn are influenced by the individual cases of the patients. It would be great if these images could be used to train a general AI model to better detect tumors. But these images can't just be sent to a central location for privacy reasons. This is where federated learning comes into play. Instead of sending the images, the training of the model remains in the respective hospital. Only the general findings - i.e. how good the model is at tumor detection - are sent back to a central location and combined there. This protects the patient's privacy.

Personalized advertising

Take an online department store as an example. If the department store wants to understand which products are of interest to which customers, they could train an AI model based on the user's browsing and purchasing behavior. With federated learning, they can train this model directly on the user's computer or smartphone. The user's specific data never leaves their device, only the model's "learning progress" is sent back to the department store. This means that personalized advertising can be offered without exceeding data protection limits.

Voice recognition and assistance systems

Imagine you have a smart speaker at home. You ask it about the weather, ask it to play music and maybe even ask it to help you cook. Your speaker gradually learns your preferences and the way you speak. Federated learning makes it possible for all these personal adjustments to take place directly on the device. Your specific data does not need to be uploaded to a cloud, which increases privacy.

Facial recognition and surveillance

A shopping center wants to increase security and uses facial recognition. The question is how to do this without invading people's privacy. Federated learning would allow the various cameras to train their models locally so that personal data does not have to be stored centrally. Only the findings about conspicuous activities could then be sent to a central location for evaluation.

In all of these examples, Differential Privacy can add an extra layer of security. Imagine you are a painter and your painting is almost finished. But before you show it to the world, you deliberately add a few small splashes of color. These splashes of color don't drastically change the overall picture, but they make it unique and not directly attributable. This is how differential privacy works. Adding a "noise" to the data ensures that the information remains anonymous. For example, a little "noise" could be added to MRI images in a hospital before they are used for training purposes, so that no one can find out which patient the image belongs to.

The great advantage of both technologies is that they make it possible to gain valuable insights from large amounts of data without jeopardizing the privacy of individuals. They are, so to speak, the "data protection officers" in the world of artificial intelligence and big data.

Both methods are still the subject of intensive research and development, but they are becoming increasingly important. Companies and organizations are beginning to realize that protecting privacy is not only ethically right, but also an important selling point. Because when people know their data is secure, they have more confidence in the technology and are more willing to use it.

Quantum computing and AI:

The combination of quantum computing and AI has the potential to increase computing power and solve complex problems that are not possible with conventional computers.

Let's first take a closer look at the term "quantum computing". A quantum computer is a very special type of computer that does not work with conventional "bits", which can only take the values 0 or 1. Instead, it uses "qubits" that can represent a combination of these values in different states at the same time. It's as if you weren't just watching black and white television, but suddenly had a whole palette of colors. This opens up completely new possibilities and makes quantum computers extremely powerful for certain tasks.

Now to AI, or artificial intelligence. AI systems are computer programs that can perform tasks that normally require human intelligence, such as recognizing language, making decisions or analyzing large amounts of data.

Well, what happens when we combine these two technologies?

The answer is simple: it could trigger a revolution in data processing and analysis.

Imagine you have a very, very large puzzle, so large that it could fill an entire soccer field. A conventional computer would probably take years to solve this puzzle. An AI system might be able to do it faster, but it would still be limited by the power of the computer it's running on. A quantum computer, however, could run through the number of possible combinations extremely quickly and thus solve the puzzle in a time that would be unthinkable using conventional methods.

Here are some advantages and application scenarios to highlight the potential of this combination:

Accelerated data processing: Quantum computers can solve tasks significantly faster than traditional computers. They have the ability to solve complex problems that are beyond the reach of conventional computers. This acceleration is crucial for the further development of AI, especially in combination with other technologies such as nanotechnology. Special programs that previously had to run in isolation, such as image recognition, speech recognition and process planning, can be combined into one program with quantum computing.

Unsupervised machine learning: The method of "unsupervised machine learning" is extended by quantum computing. In this method, neural network algorithms recognize and interpret raw data without any training. They should be able to recognize correlations themselves, learn from experience and correct their own mistakes, just like humans. The possibilities and complexity arising from quantum computing cannot yet be fully assessed, but they open up exciting new avenues for AI.

Processing large amounts of data: The combination of AI and quantum computing makes it possible to process large fields of data in a single step, discover patterns in the data that classical computers cannot, and work with incomplete or uncertain data. When developing AI models for specific applications such as drug development or climate modeling, quantum computers could perform complex simulations that are out of reach for traditional computers. This capability could be crucial in creating more realistic models and making better predictions.

Advanced pattern recognition: Quantum computers have the ability to work in superposition, which could allow multiple data paths to be analyzed simultaneously. This property could lead to more precise and in-depth pattern recognition, which would be beneficial for many AI applications such as image and speech recognition.

Possibility of new algorithms: By supporting research and development, quantum computers could help develop novel AI algorithms and architectures that were previously unthinkable. This could drive a new wave of innovation in AI technology and advance the field

Exponential storage capacity: Quantum computers utilize the exponential nature of quantum systems. In contrast to classical systems, where the storage capacity lies in the individual data units, the majority of the storage capacity of a quantum system lies in the collective properties of the qubits (the basic units of quantum computing

Of course, we are still a long way from fully exploiting all these possibilities. Both quantum computers and AI systems are extremely complex technologies that are still in their infancy. There are technical challenges, ethical concerns and, of course, the question of cost. But the

first steps have been taken and research in this field is progressing
rapidly.

A look into the future

If we look 30 years into the future, we can expect a very advanced form of AI. During this time, AI could not only take on specialized tasks, but also very complex and creative ones. To illustrate this better, I would like to give an example: The AI doctors of the future.

Imagine you don't feel well and decide to go to the doctor. You enter the doctor's office and instead of a human doctor, you sit down in front of a computer screen. This AI doctor asks you about your symptoms and within a few seconds performs millions of calculations. It accesses all of humanity's medical knowledge, compares your symptoms with similar cases, draws on the latest scientific findings and finally gives you a diagnosis.

What's particularly interesting here is that this AI could even be able to develop new treatments by accessing information from medical research, clinical trials and even other specialties. It might discover that a drug originally developed for another disease could work wonders for your particular condition. This is, of course, a very positive view of the future and could revolutionize healthcare.

Ecological sustainability

One of the biggest challenges posed by AI development is the sustainability aspect. AI systems, especially the advanced ones, can consume enormous amounts of energy. It is therefore crucial that we use renewable energy sources. It is not enough to simply push the technology forward; we must also consider the impact on our planet.

In addition, the hardware on which the AI runs should be made from sustainable materials. As more and more computers and servers are needed for the ongoing development of AI, we need to ensure that this hardware is not only powerful but also environmentally friendly. This applies to the extraction of materials, the production process and finally the recycling of the hardware.

Social impact

Another important aspect is the social impact of AI. We need to ensure that the benefits of AI are widely distributed throughout society and not just to a small elite. There is a risk that jobs could be lost through the use of AI, which is why education and retraining play a major role.

Imagine a society where everyone has access to AI-based education. Here, AI could create personalized learning plans for each student so that everyone has the same opportunities. But what happens if only wealthy schools can afford such systems? Then the gap between rich and poor would continue to grow.

Economic implications

Advances in AI will also have a massive economic impact. If machines and algorithms take over more and more human activities, many traditional professions could become obsolete. That sounds scary at first, but it also offers opportunities for new fields of work.

Let's take agriculture as an example. A few decades ago, it would have been hard to imagine that robots could do most of the agricultural work. But in 30 years' time, a farmer could use AI to optimize his harvest, choose the best time to sow and even have weeds removed automatically. These technologies could help to combat hunger in the world.

But of course the question also arises: what will happen to the people who have worked in agriculture up to now? This is where politics plays a decisive role. A socially acceptable transition with educational programs and retraining measures is crucial.

Psychological effects

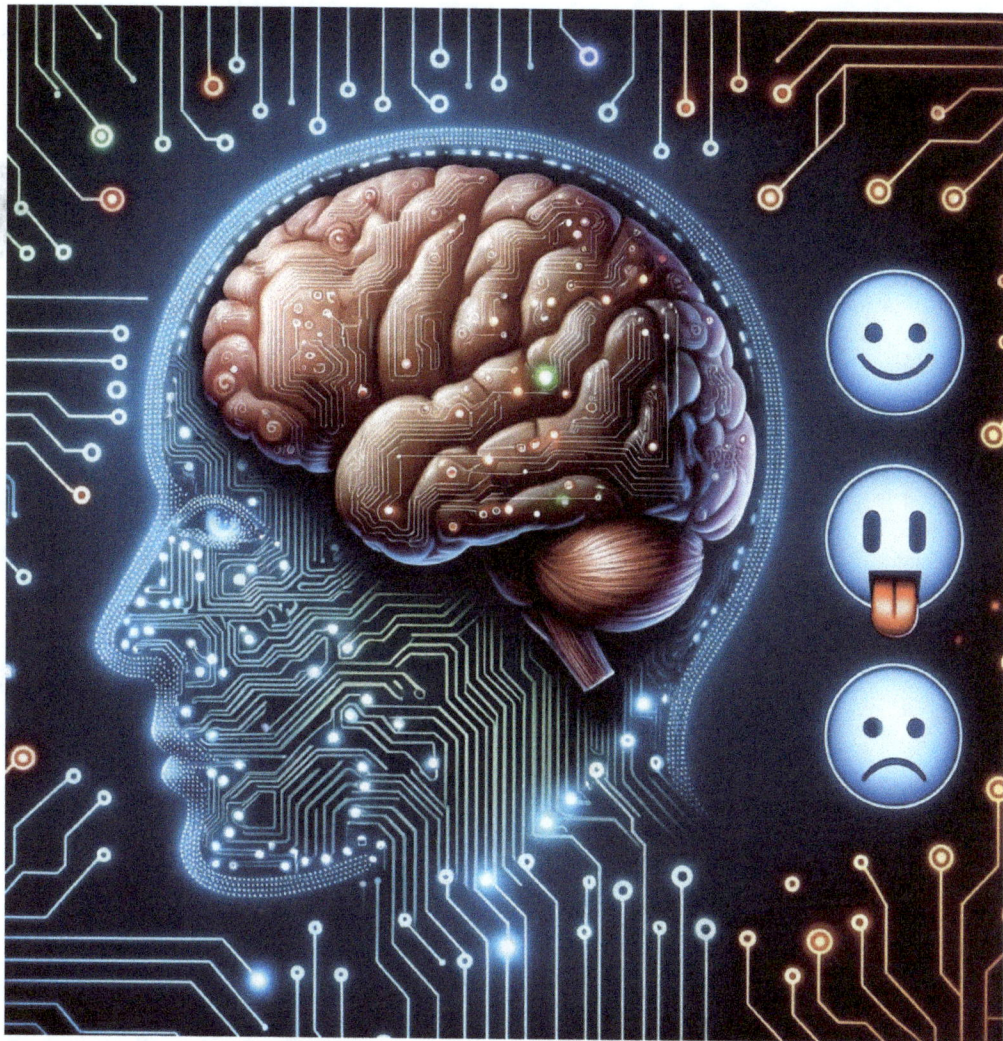

The psychological impact of AI is another topic that is often overlooked. When AI systems take over human-like tasks, it will change our relationship with technology and perhaps even with ourselves. Imagine having an AI assistant that is so good that it can recognize your moods and anticipate your needs. This could change our understanding of human interaction and pose new ethical questions.

It could well be that in 30 years' time, AI systems will be so advanced that they could act as therapists. These AI therapists could always be available and have access to extensive databases of psychological knowledge. But what does this mean for the doctor-patient relationship, which is based on trust? Could we really trust a machine?

AI and art

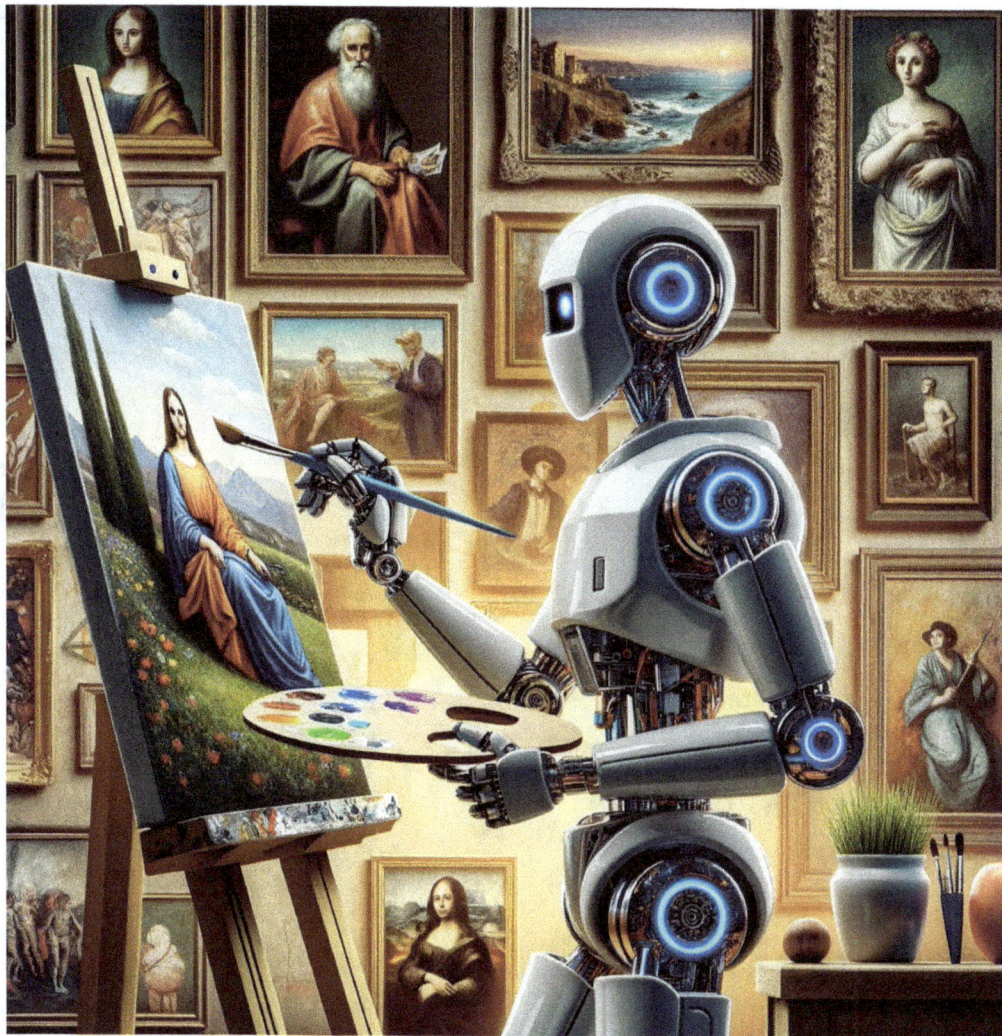

Another exciting field is art. AI systems could not only analyze works of art, but also produce creative works themselves. These technologies could give rise to new forms of art that we cannot even imagine today.

Imagine an AI writing a novel. It could analyze thousands of books in milliseconds and write a text that is both exciting and profound. But would we consider such a work to be "real" art? And what would that mean for human artists?

Global competition

One aspect that should not be forgotten is global competition. Countries and companies are already vying for supremacy in the field of AI. Whoever comes out on top here could enjoy considerable advantages both economically and geopolitically. International cooperation is therefore important to prevent an "AI arms race".

Regulation and legislation

The government has the task of creating a legal framework for the use of AI in good time. How about, for example, a kind of "AI TÜV", an independent institution that ensures that AI systems are safe and ethical? This institution could carry out tests and audits and issue certificates for AI systems that meet certain requirements.

Human-machine interaction

The interaction between humans and AI systems is expected to become increasingly seamless and intuitive. We may reach a point where the distinction between human capabilities and what an AI can do becomes increasingly blurred.

Imagine there is an AI system that can translate not only language but also emotions in real time. So when you speak to someone who speaks a different language, the AI could convey not only the words but also the emotional context. This could fundamentally change the way we communicate and build relationships. But it also raises ethical questions. For example, should AI be able to 'censor' or alter emotions?

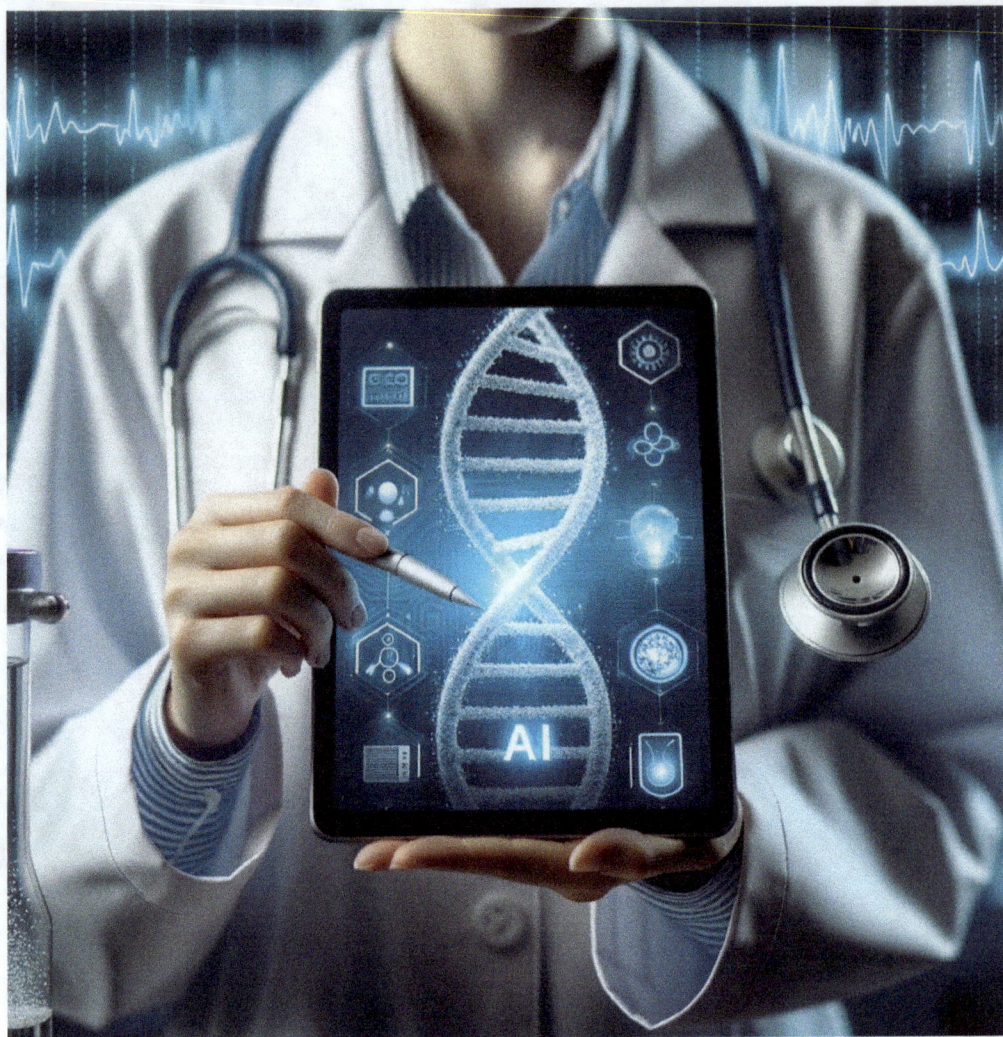

Another exciting area is that of health and longevity. With the help of AI, we could begin to better understand the human ageing process and perhaps even slow it down.

An AI system could analyze countless scientific studies and biological data to find new ways to slow down the aging process. This technology could enable us to live longer and healthier lives. But of course, this also raises ethical and societal questions, for example with regard to population density and the earth's resources.

AI in governance

The use of AI in administration and governance could also be a revolution. AI systems could help to make decisions based on an enormous amount of data and thus contribute to more efficient and fairer social systems.

For example, the AI could design a tax system that is so complex and individualized that it calculates the fairest and most efficient tax burden for each citizen. The AI could take into account factors such as income, living circumstances, personal expenses and much more. But of course there are ethical considerations here too. Would people want to give a machine the power to make such important decisions?

Cyber security

With the growing reliance on AI systems, cyber security is also becoming increasingly important. Advanced AI could be both a threat and a solution in this area.

A country could develop an AI that is capable of outwitting the defense systems of another country. At the same time, the defending country could have an AI that fends off such attacks in real time. This could lead to a never-ending race between AI systems in which the stability of the global order is at stake.

How AI is developed and deployed has a significant impact on social justice. Discrimination and prejudice can be reinforced by poorly designed or biased AI systems.

Imagine an AI system being used to predict crime. If this system is trained on historical data that is already discriminatory, it could reinforce prejudices and unfairly disadvantage certain social or ethnic groups. This could perpetuate and exacerbate unjust social structures, which poses a significant ethical problem.

Autonomy and self-determination

As AI develops, our autonomy and sense of self-determination could be compromised. AI systems could become so good at predicting human behavior that they could effectively control our decisions.

Suppose an AI knows your likes and dislikes so well that it can suggest products or services to you that you can hardly resist. This raises the question of the extent to which we can still act as autonomous, self-determined individuals if a machine can predict our decisions better than we can.

Conclusion: An integrated approach for the future of AI

Artificial intelligence is on the brink of a turning point that could fundamentally reshape our society over the next 30 years. The challenges are as complex as the opportunities are impressive. It is not just about making technological advances, but also about considering the ethical, social and environmental implications of this technology.

The shaping of this AI future cannot lie solely in the hands of technicians, scientists or entrepreneurs. It requires a broad societal debate and the collaboration of experts from ethics, social sciences, law and many other disciplines. All of us, young and old, must have the opportunity to take part in this discussion and express our concerns and hopes.

Governments have a crucial role to play in controlling and regulating AI development. They must ensure that laws and regulations both promote innovation and protect citizens from abuse. It is important that legislation is not only nationally but also internationally coordinated in order to be effective.

The pursuit of sustainable AI must be in line with global sustainability goals. In addition to technological development, this also means taking into account the responsible use of resources and not further increasing social inequalities.

The industry must be aware of the responsibility it bears in the development and implementation of AI technologies. This means not only setting down ethical principles on paper, but also implementing them consistently in practice.

As AI will revolutionize many professional fields, lifelong learning is crucial for all age groups. Everyone must have the opportunity to continue their education and adapt to changing professional requirements.

Ultimately, it is about finding a balance between the enormous opportunities and the equally great risks of AI. This is no easy task, but it is feasible if all stakeholders - scientists, politicians, citizens and the AI systems themselves - work together in an integrated manner.

The path to the future is complex and full of uncertainties, but also full of opportunities. With a collective effort that recognizes the complexity of the challenges and addresses them holistically, we can hope to shape an AI future that is not only technologically advanced, but also ethically justifiable and socially equitable. And that is a future we should all be working towards.

In the final chapter of this book, we want to reveal a special secret to you: All the images you encountered while leafing through the pages were not created by an artist or photographer, but by an artificial intelligence. This artificial intelligence is called DALLE-3 and we would like to briefly show you the process behind it:

Instructions for activating DALL-E 3

To unleash the full potential of ChatGPT, the book provides step-by-step instructions and real-world examples. Here is a basic guide to installing plugins, the code interpreter and DALL-E 3 in GPT-4:

Note: This guide was written in 10/2023 and is based on the ChatGPT features of the ChatGPT September 25 release. In addition, a ChatGPT Plus account is currently required to use all the features listed below.

First of all, there is one step that you only need to take once with your ChatGPT Plus account: Click on the three dots at the bottom left to open the menu. Then select "Beta functions" and then activate "Plugins" and "Code interpreter". (Note: DALL-E 3 also works without this first step)

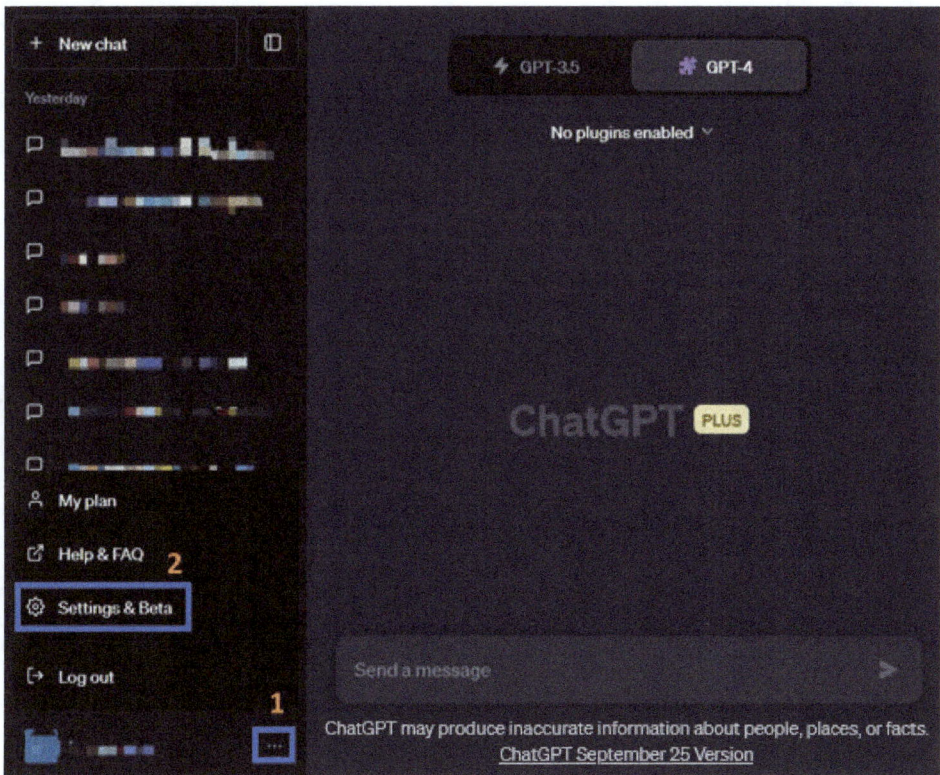

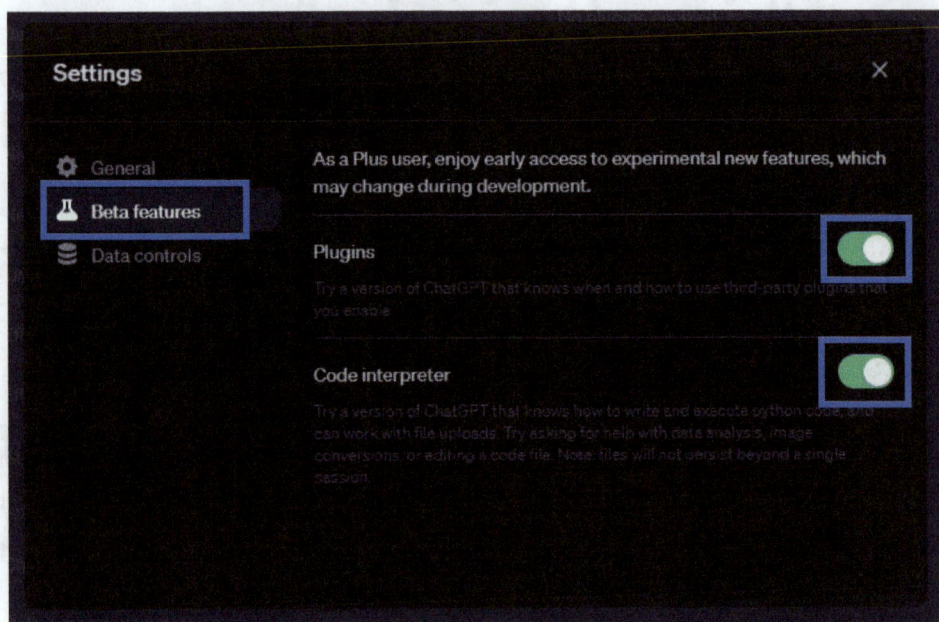

To activate DALL-E 3, certain plugins or the code interpreter, you must start a new chat with ChatGPT. Select GPT-4 and in the drop-down menu for GPT-4 you then have the option of activating either DALL-E 3, the code interpreter or the plugins.

⚡ GPT-3.5 | 🤖 GPT-4 ∧

Our most capable model, great for tasks that require creativity and advanced reasoning.

Available exclusively to Plus users

GPT-4 currently has a cap of 50 messages every 3 hours.

✦ Default

🌐 Browse with ᵇ Bing Beta

🖼 Advanced Data Analysis Beta

✳ Plugins Beta

🖼 DALL·E 3 Beta   ✓

| Brainstorm names | Come up with concepts |
| for a non-alcoholic cocktail with Co... | for a retro-style arcade game |

Send a message   ➤

ChatGPT may produce inaccurate information about people, places, or facts. ChatGPT September 25 Version

In the following, we will show you how we created the images used in this book. With a few tricks, you can quickly achieve great results with good and precise prompts. We will explain how this works in detail in a separate book. After this chapter, we will show you which books will take your use of ChatGPT to the next level.

Our input in ChatGPT:

Introduction: A photo showing an open book page. The page emits a soft, warm light that illuminates the space around the book. Stylized circuits and binary code can be seen on the book page, symbolizing the connection between literature and technology.

Output ChatGPT:

Looking back: An oil painting depicting an ancient library. In the center of the picture is a large telescope pointed at the sky. This symbolizes the human urge to look beyond the horizon and seek new knowledge.

Early beginnings: A photo showing an old, dusty workshop. Various mechanical parts and simple tools lie on a workbench. A simple robotic arm from the early days of robotics tries to grasp a cube.

1950s: The birth: A drawing showing a group of scientists in a laboratory in the 1950s. They are working on large computers with lots of cables and flashing lights. One of the scientists points to a screen on which the first AI algorithm is running.

1960s and 1970s: First successes and setbacks: A photo showing a collage of newspaper articles and magazines from the 1960s and 1970s. The headlines are about the first successes of AI, but also about the challenges and setbacks during this time.

1990s: The Internet and more data: An illustration depicting the world as a globe surrounded by computer monitors. The monitors show various websites, and data streams flow from the monitors to the globe. This symbolizes the explosion of the Internet and the increase in data that influenced AI research.

Today: AI in everyday life: a photo depicting modern everyday life. People of different genders and backgrounds are using smartphones, smartwatches and other technologies. Autonomous vehicles and robots can be seen in the background performing everyday tasks.

Definition: What is artificial intelligence? A drawing showing a pair of scales. On one side of the scale is a human brain, on the other a computer chip. A light bulb hovers above the scales, symbolizing the moment of understanding and enlightenment.

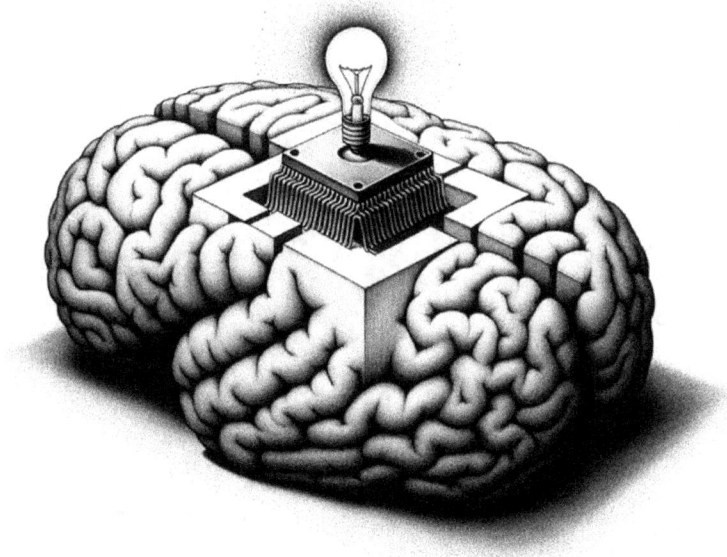

Narrow AI: An illustration showing a machine that performs specific tasks perfectly, such as playing chess or making weather forecasts. People of different genders and backgrounds stand around the machine and marvel at its abilities, while other machines that fail in other areas are shown in the background.

Strong AI (General AI): An oil painting depicting a futuristic city. Robots and humans of different genders and backgrounds live and work together harmoniously. The robots display human-like emotions and abilities.

Super intelligent AI (Super AI): A photo showing a huge computer in a modern data center. The computer emits a bright light and is networked with many other machines. People of different genders and backgrounds stand around the computer in awe.

Lighthouses of Thought: Wisdom and Warnings from the World of AI: A watercolor painting depicting an old sage sitting on a mountaintop looking down at the valley below. In his hand he holds a book entitled "AI" and holographic images of quotes and wisdom fly around him.

Current trends: The picture shows a conference or trade fair on the subject of AI, where people of different genders and backgrounds are looking at the latest AI innovations.

Machine learning on the edge (Edge AI): The illustration depicts a modern smart device with microscopic circuits visible inside. This symbolizes the concept of "edge computing".

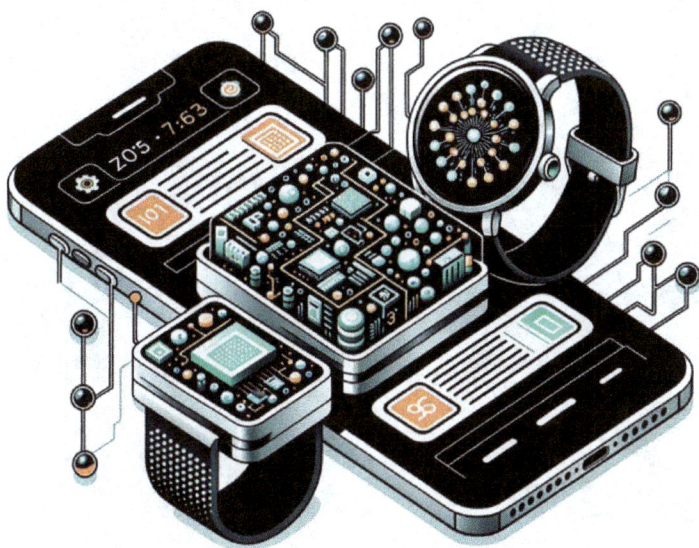

Self-monitoring learning: The oil painting shows an AI reflecting itself in a mirror and learning in the process.

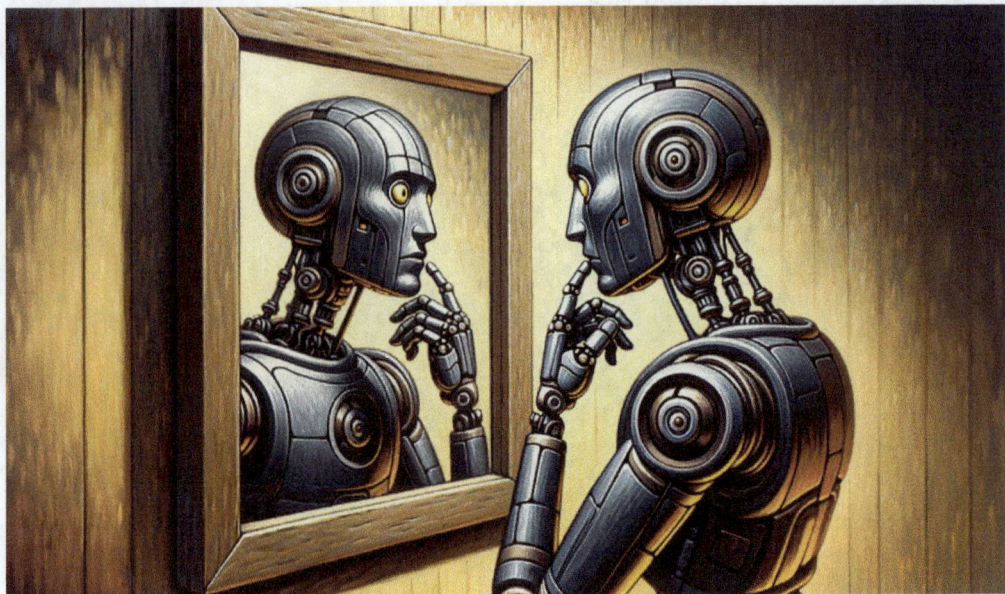

Transfer Learning: In the drawing, a robot teaches another robot by transferring information via a cable. People of different genders and backgrounds observe this process.

Next generation language models: A photo showing a modern, open workplace. People of different genders and backgrounds are sitting in front of their computers wearing headphones. Chatbots and speech recognition programs can be seen on their screens. Hovering above them is a holographic representation of waveforms and speech patterns.

AI for sustainability: The illustration depicts a green, thriving city where people plant trees and use sustainable technologies.

Explainability and transparency of AI: The oil painting shows an AI in the form of a glass robot. People stand around the robot and study it attentively.

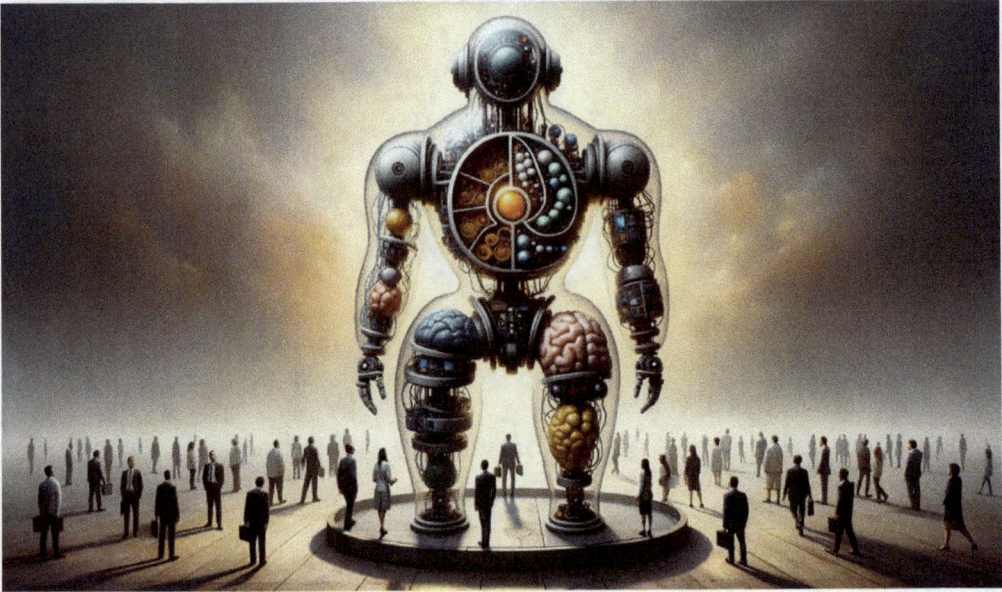

Augmented reality and AI: The photo shows a group of people wearing special glasses and experiencing augmented reality.

Robotics and autonomous systems: A photo showing a modern factory floor. Robotic arms of various shapes and sizes carry out precise tasks. People of different genders and backgrounds monitor the processes and interact with the robots via tablets and computers.

Excursus: Multimodal systems: An illustration depicting a central AI system that is connected to various sensors such as cameras, microphones and touch sensors. The system processes different input formats simultaneously and performs coordinated actions.

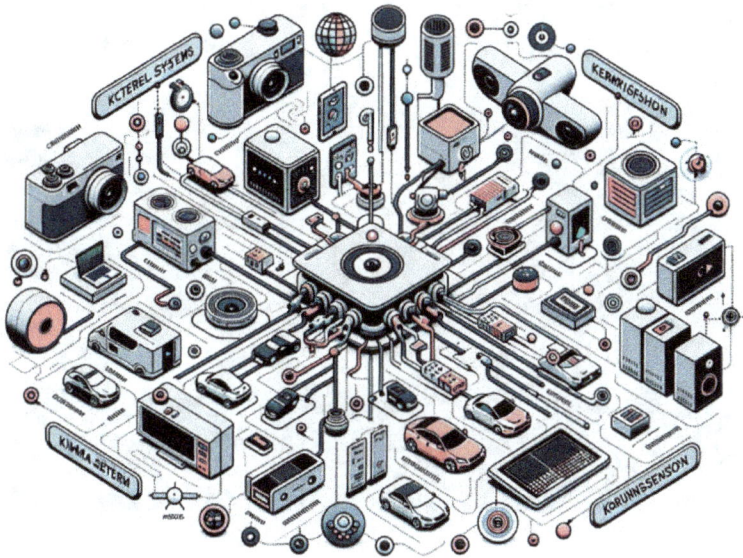

Data protection and AI: The oil painting depicts a safe in which data is represented in the form of glowing cubes. A robotic arm is trying to gain access, but is blocked by a data protection shield.

Quantum computing and AI: The drawing shows a futuristic computer surrounded by energetic waves that people observe with interest.

A look into the future: an illustration depicting a futuristic city at night. The skyline is characterized by glowing, tall buildings. Autonomous vehicles and drones hover above the city. People of different genders and backgrounds walk on busy streets and interact with holographic displays.

Ecological sustainability: A photo of a green plant growing from a computer chip to illustrate the connection between technology and nature. In the background is a diagram showing ethical principles.

Social impact: A photo of a diverse group of people all looking at their smartphones while holographic icons for various social networks float in the background.

Economic implications: A photo of a modern city with skyscrapers, with one of the skyscrapers looking like a giant robotic arm stacking coins.

Psychological impact: An illustration of a human brain connected to digital circuits, and next to it emotional symbols such as a laughing face and a sad face.

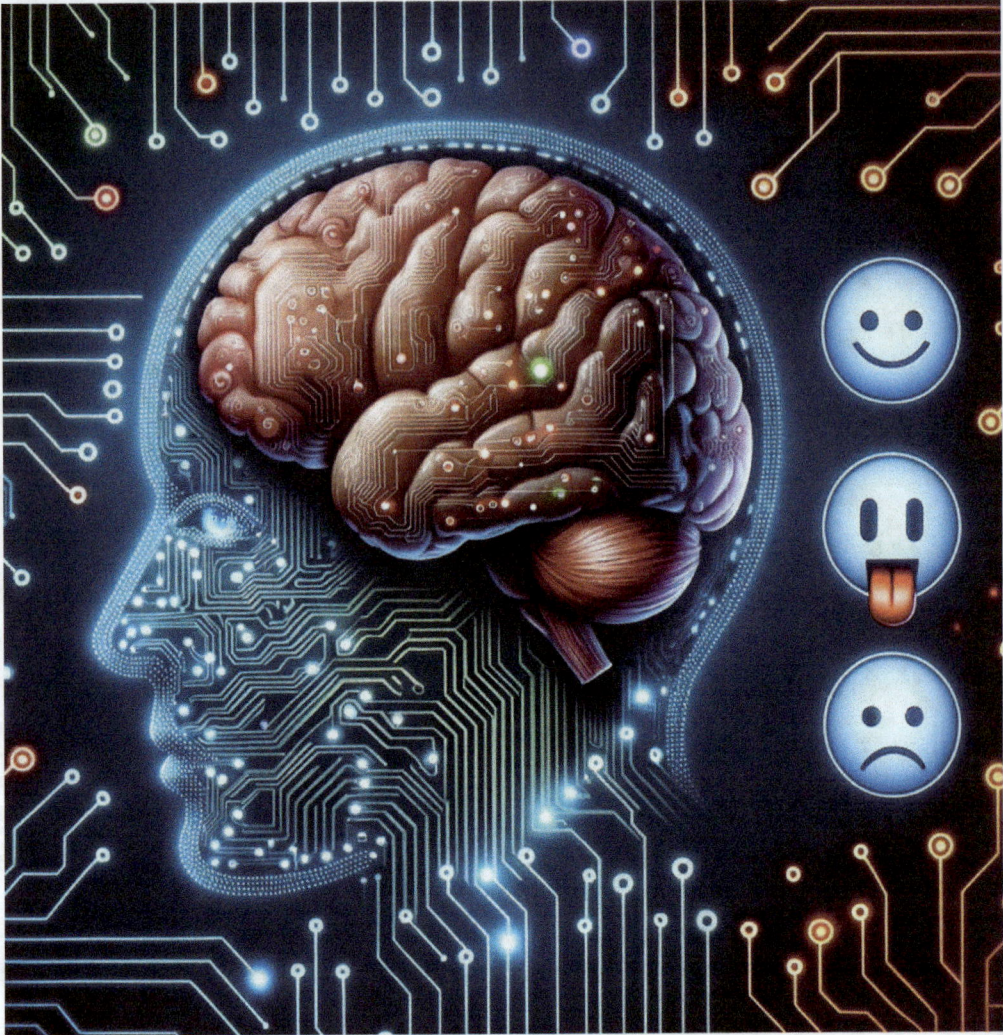

AI and art: An oil painting of a robot painting at an easel, while classical and modern works of art can be seen in the background.

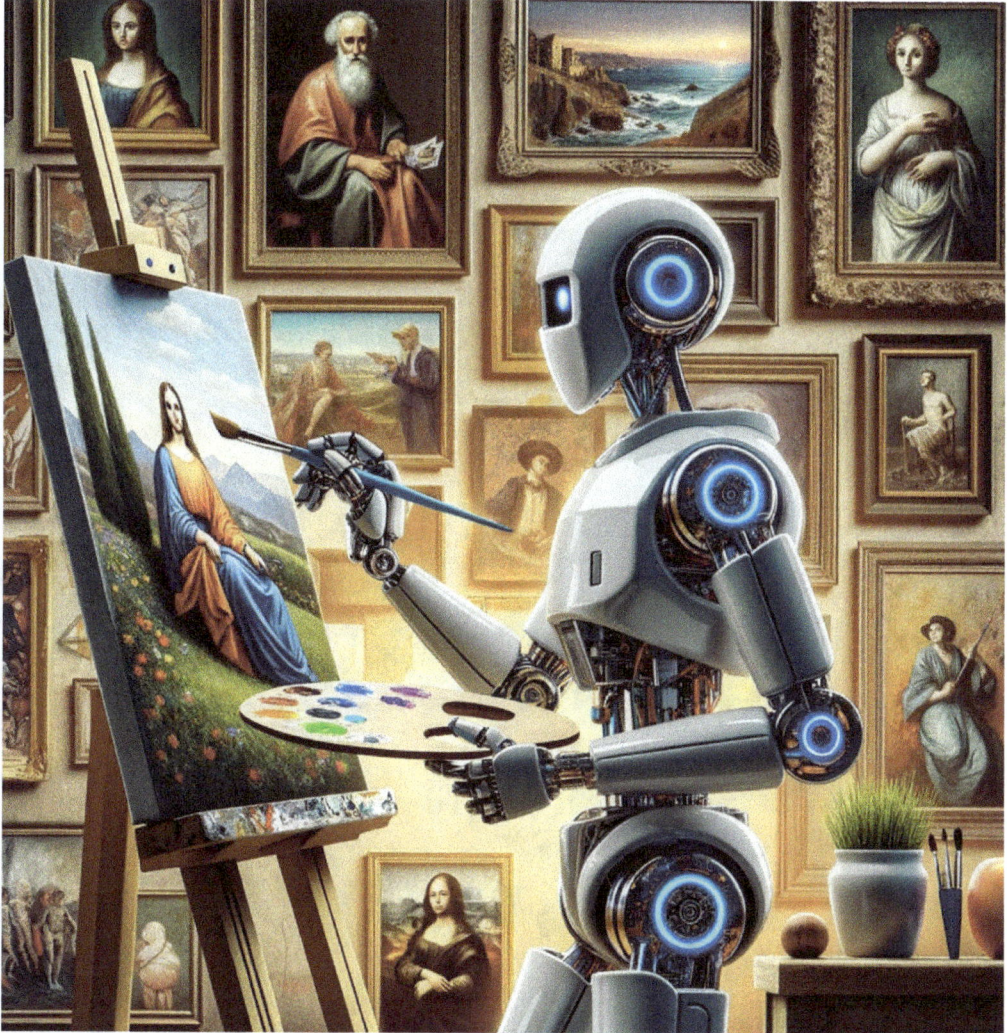

Global competition: The picture shows an international athletics event in a busy arena. Runners of different nationalities race on a track while the audience in the background cheers with national flags. A glowing world map adorns the background and symbolizes global participation.

Regulation and legislation: The image shows a high-tech room full of people at futuristic workstations, surrounded by floating holographic representations and glowing displays.

Human-machine interaction: A drawing of a human and a robot shaking hands, while symbols for various technologies float in the background.

Health and longevity: A photo of a doctor holding a tablet on which an AI application can be seen. DNA strands and medical devices are shown in the background.

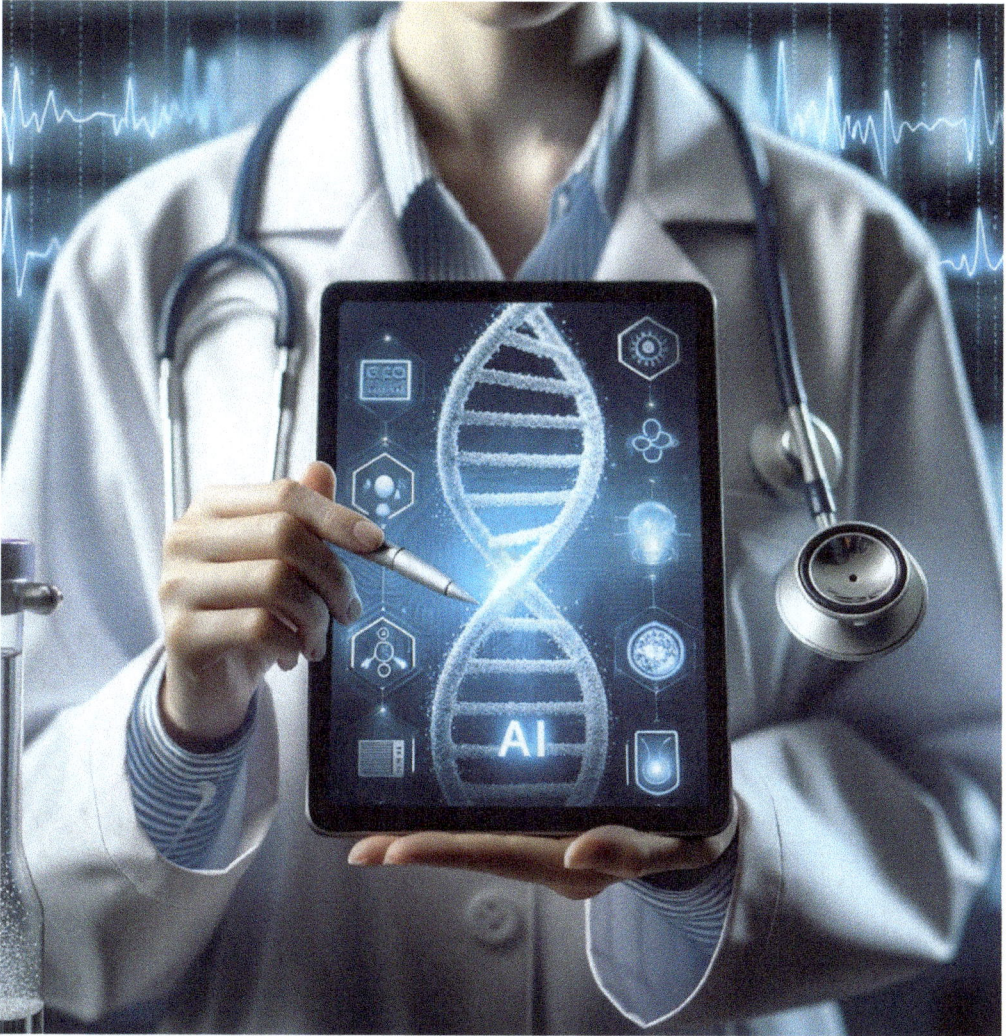

AI in governance: An illustration of a government building in front of which robots and humans are demonstrating together, with banners saying "AI for all" and "Just AI".

Cyber security: A photo of a lock symbol on a digital background, surrounded by binary code and warning symbols.

Social justice and AI: A drawing of a scale with a robot on one side and various people on the other to represent the balance between technology and humanity.

Autonomy and self-determination: A photo of a person wearing VR goggles while navigating through a digital landscape showing symbols of freedom and freedom of choice.

Summary: An integrated approach for the future of AI: A photo showing a group of people in a bright conference room. They are having a lively discussion and pointing at a large screen on which various AI concepts are visualized. The room radiates an atmosphere of collaboration and optimism.

So, next time you flick through this book and come across one of the images, remember: behind every picture is a fascinating technology that is increasingly blurring the boundaries between man and machine. It's an exciting time we live in, isn't it?

If you want to delve deeper into the world of artificial intelligence and understand how you can use it in your job, in self-employment or for other special applications, then we recommend our other books.

Our other books cover a variety of topics and offer practical guidance on how to harness the power of artificial intelligence for your own purposes. Each book is designed not only to provide you with theoretical knowledge, but also to give you concrete tools that you can apply immediately in your professional or personal life.

So, if you want to take the next step into this exciting world of technology, take a look at our other publications. It could be the start of a fascinating journey.

Your way to become a prompt expert!

A comprehensive guide for working with ChatGPT

The future of writing

The Ultimate Guide to Academic Writing with ChatGPT

Your Guide to ChatGPT Superpowers

Plugins 101

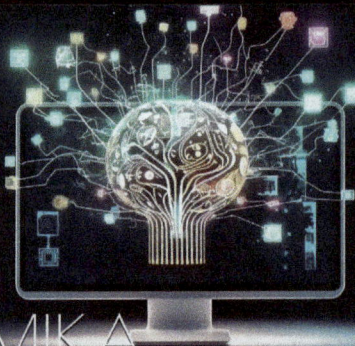

MIKA SCHWAN

MIKA SCHWAN

Building a side hustle

Intelligence, Innovation, 1.000.000 $

The AI path to financial freedom

UTILIZE THE POWER OF ARTIFICIAL INTELLIGENCE TO BOOST YOUR INCOME AND PREPARE YOURSELF FOR THE WORKFORCE OF TOMORROW!

Image sources

ChatGPT - OpenAI (http://chat.openai.com/), last accessed on October 24, 2023.

Our thanks for your trust

Dear reader,

Thank you for your support and interest in our book on artificial intelligence. We are glad that we could share our experiences and insights with you. We hope the book helps you to understand AI better and use it more effectively.

It has been a pleasure to share our insights and experiences with you in this book and we hope that it has helped you to develop a deeper understanding of the subject.

If you would like to stay up to date with our work in the field of artificial intelligence, you are welcome to sign up for our e-mail newsletter. (https://bit.ly/3Uautfo)

Thank you again for your support and we hope to see you again in the future.

 Alternative registration for the newsletter via the QR code:

Thank you again for your support and we hope to see you again in the future.

Imprint

Texts: © Copyright by Mika Schwan, Lucas Greif and Andreas Kimmig

Cover design: © Copyright by Mika Schwan, Lucas Greif and Andreas Kimmig

Publisher:

GbR with Lucas Greif, Andreas Kimmig, Philipp Lepold, Mika Schwan

Kuppeheimerstrasse 6

76476 Bischweier

mlap4life@gmail.com

9 7 9 8 8 7 0 2 6 9 0 5 4